UPDATED EDITION

KITCHEN IDEAS YOU CAN USE

The Latest Styles, Appliances, Features, and Tips
for Renovating Your Kitchen

CHRIS PETERSON

COOL
SPRINGS
PRESS

Inspiring | Educating | Creating | Entertaining

Brimming with creative inspiration, how-to projects, and useful information to enrich your everyday life, Quarto Knows is a favorite destination for those pursuing their interests and passions. Visit our site and dig deeper with our books into your area of interest: Quarto Creates, Quarto Cooks, Quarto Homes, Quarto Lives, Quarto Drives, Quarto Explores, Quarto Gifts, or Quarto Kids.

10 9 8 7 6 5 4 3 2 1

ISBN: 978-0-7603-6067-5

Library of Congress Cataloging-in-Publication Data

Names: Peterson, Chris, 1961- author.
Title: Kitchen ideas you can use : the latest styles, appliances, features
   and tips for renovating your kitchen / Chris Peterson.
Description: Updated edition. | Minneapolis, MN, USA : Cool Springs Press, an
   imprint of The Quarto Group, [2018] | Includes bibliographical references.
Identifiers: LCCN 2017049409 | ISBN 9780760360675 (pb)
Subjects: LCSH: Kitchens--Remodeling. | Kitchens--Design and construction.
Classification: LCC TH4816.3.K58 P475 2018 | DDC 747.7/97--dc23
LC record available at https://lccn.loc.gov/2017049409

Acquiring Editor: Mark Johanson
Project Manager: Nyle Vialet
Art Director: Brad Springer
Cover & Interior Design: Amy Sly

Printed in China

Contents

INTRODUCTION

Kitchens continue to be the social centers of most homes. That hasn't changed for decades. But the space in which all that socializing happens has changed, and continues to evolve. This updated edition of *Kitchen Ideas You Can Use* pays homage to that evolution, and describes the ways in which today's homeowners are creating unique, beautiful, and multifaceted kitchens.

You'll find that there are few earthshaking changes in kitchen design. "Smart" home spaces may grab headlines, but refrigerators that can monitor their contents and order milk when you need it are still far from common or widespread. Technology is not the kitchen game-changer that home magazines might make it out to be. The most important things we do in the room—cooking, eating, and interacting with one another—still remain low-tech, but eminently satisfying. Most homeowners are not looking to make those activities more complex. Rather, they continue to want the space to accommodate everything that happens in the room, or they want the space to be a beautiful, welcoming, functional, and fun room in the house.

That's why the latest developments in kitchen design focus on small changes that can have big impact on the day-to-day use of the room.

▼ **PLAY WITH PATTERN.** Pattern adds excitement and energy to any kitchen, but should be used in small doses so that it doesn't overwhelm the space and become too visually busy. This backsplash tile breaks up the look of sophisticated solid-color cabinets and countertops, with three types of polished marble tile forming a flowing diamond grid. The look grabs the eye, but not to the detriment of other decorative elements.

For instance, bold lighting fixtures are playing an increasingly important role in home kitchens across the country. Where once we sought to hide light sources, now they're taking center stage in forms that are as exciting as anything you'll find in the rest of the house. Of course, for all their visual interest, those fixtures still must meet the needs specific to a kitchen. Fortunately, lighting manufacturers have developed entire lines around beautiful kitchen illumination that feature newer earth-friendly options like LEDs.

You'll also find new surface alternatives that bring a fresh approach to kitchen counters, backsplashes, and floors. The popularity of quartz—and the ever-increasing number of looks that particular material offers—is just one example. Tiles painted in intricate and colorful patterns are finding a home on kitchen floors, as backsplashes, and even as countertops. Because they are so many possibilities, designers are increasingly mixing countertop materials. It's an easy way for any homeowner to not only freshen the look of her kitchen, but to add even more visual interest along the way.

Function is also being refined in the kitchen, most specifically in the area of storage. You won't have to look far to find incredibly specialized storage options, whether you need to keep a passel of utensils in order, want to fill a large drawer with special china, or just need to get some control over your spices and other pantry goods.

But ultimately, today's kitchen is all about the intersection of comfort and beauty. The pages that follow present a wealth of examples of life lived at that intersection.

◀ **IMPRESS WITH SUBTLE ELEGANCE.** You don't necessarily need bold colors or sleek surfaces to create a killer kitchen design. Here, accents like a gooseneck faucet and island-mounted pot filler accent the sophisticated cream-colored cabinets and the matching face panels on the refrigerator. The butcher-block, marble counters, and inset cooktop drive home the point that this is a serious cook's kitchen, but one with a refined aesthetic sense.

▶ **USE YOUR APPLIANCES TO MAKE A STATEMENT.** There's no excuse for dull appliances in a newly designed or renovated kitchen. Today, manufacturers offer units that combine exceptional function with unusual looks. This glass-front refrigerator is just one example, but a sleek one that makes sense for a stunning cooking-oriented kitchen. You get a peek in at what's on offer without ever opening the door— translating to energy savings and a cool visual.

EXPERIMENT WITH KITCHEN COLOR BY PAINTING THE WALLS. Muted kitchen colors are all the rage, but fashion and tastes change, and paint can change with them. Notice how well this particular color works with the elegant granite counters and the traditional, raised-panel, framed cabinets. The cabinets feature a rich maple finish that would complement a wide range of colors, and the same is true of the stainless steel appliances.

▲ **CREATE A PERSONALIZED ACCENT WITH A BACKSPLASH.** Here, fun and colorful mosaic glass tile creates an upbeat look that brings a little zest to the otherwise stately look of a stainless steel hood, professional-quality range, and traditional cabinets. Backsplashes are the dream canvases of a kitchen, where you can get a bit wild without risking too much.

▲ **FINISH THE PICTURE OF YOUR KITCHEN DESIGN WITH FINELY CRAFTED DETAILS LIKE THESE SLEEK MODERN HANDLES.** They may not call attention to themselves, but they are the height of elegance, and the perfect complement to reclaimed-wood cabinets. The wonderful thing about sophisticated, artsy pulls or knobs like these is that they deliver a great deal of visual appeal without having an oversized impact on your wallet.

▶ **USE LIGHT FIXTURES AS SIGNATURE DESIGN ELEMENTS.** The amazing lighting options offered by today's manufacturers ensure you can find eye-catching fixtures to suit any kitchen style. Or you can pick a fixture like this spectacular example, one that sets the tone for the rest of the kitchen. This "chandelier" features 26 crystal disks powered by xenon lights and a sandblasted design. On or off, it's a showstopper centerpiece for the kitchen.

▶ **WARM IT WITH WOOD.** Where wood floors were once unthinkable in the kitchen, they are now a surface of choice. No wonder, given the amazing diversity of wood types, grain patterns, plank widths, and stains. The midtone hickory in this kitchen is a timeless look that will add luster to the space for decades. That longevity is also part of wood's allure. Most wood floors only gain character with time and wear.

▲ **KEEP IT CLASSY WITH QUARTZ.** This natural quartz countertop has been crafted to mimic the look of marble without the need to for resealing and maintenance that a marble surface would require. Beautiful, durable, scratch- and stain-resistant, quartz is an excellent choice for an upscale kitchen such as this white and wonderful space.

▲ **FIT LUXURY INTO ANY SPACE.** This compact kitchen proves that you don't need a ton of square footage to create a dynamite workspace. Pro-quality appliances, including a separate fridge and freezer, and a six-burner stove, are surrounded by marble tile and countertops. A herringbone wood floor and classic shaded pendants accent the look, as do stainless-steel shelves. The room could not be more opulent or more efficiently laid out.

◀ **TURN TO MULTIFACETED FREESTANDING CABINETS FOR THE ULTIMATE IN STORAGE FLEXIBILITY.** This beautiful unit not only looks stunning with the doors closed, but it couldn't be more useful when they're open. It includes trays, drawers, cabinets, shelves, and even a work surface. This type of all-in-one cabinet can be incredibly practical in a larger kitchen, but it can also take over most of the storage and prep area needs in a small space. Open or closed, it's an elegant style that suits any kitchen.

▲ **OPT FOR ECO-FRIENDLY UPSCALE.** A bamboo island and reclaimed flagstone wall cladding are environmentally friendly design options that bring a stunning complement to luxury appliances in this kitchen. The sleek stainless steel exterior of the appliances and the sophisticated smoked-glass window fronting the wine refrigerator are perfect contrasts to the rough-hewn surface of the walls. This type of textural contrast is a great way to build visual interest in your kitchen.

▶ **THINK "UNUSUAL MATERIALS" TO CREATE CENTERPIECE SURFACES.** This work surface was custom-formed of float glass and then set into a concrete frame. This is a truly modern look, but one with an enchantingly industrial edge. Regardless of the style tag you stick on it, this idea could be adapted to many different kitchen decorating styles. The homeowner could have chosen from among a spectrum of glass colors, and the concrete can be tinted, polished to a high sheen, or even stamped with a unique surface relief.

GO MODERN ELECTRIC FOR SPECTACULAR STREAMLINED APPEARANCES. Today's induction electric cooktops give any gas units a run for their money in both looks and performance. A high-end electric cooktop like this one simply can't be topped for a sleek, minimalist look. Paired with a stunning range hood like the glass-edged model in this kitchen, a modern electric cooktop can be a big style focal point in a modern or contemporary kitchen design.

ADD A FARMHOUSE SINK FOR COUNTRY FLAIR. Country or farmhouse kitchen designs are often defined by a few key design elements, one of which is the enameled cast-iron apron-front farmhouse sink. Its distinctive profile is unmistakable, and the form of the sink provides plenty of room inside to clean and maneuver oversized pots and pans. Match the sink with a super stylish shiny chrome faucet like the traditional gooseneck unit shown here, and you have an unbeatable combination that brings a lot of pizzazz to the country kitchen.

STYLE BY SIZE

Cozy Kitchens

Family-Friendly Spaces

Large & Luxurious

Kitchen size determines just how hard you'll need to work in balancing function and form. In a smaller space, organization and layout may be the most important aspects of any redesign effort. In a large, open floor plan, you'll have a lot more latitude regarding what looks best where. But you should always keep in mind that the size of a kitchen presents design challenges and benefits—whether it is a tiny galley kitchen or a restaurant-size cooking space.

Small kitchens are about efficiency, but they also allow you to integrate ultra-luxury elements like a marble surface that you might not be able to afford if you had to cover larger surface areas. Sometimes one design feature, like an upscale refrigerator or granite backsplash, can make the look of a small kitchen.

More likely, you'll have a midsize room to work with (what are labeled "Family-Friendly Spaces" in this section). Bringing these types of kitchens to life means building efficiency and practicality into stylish design solutions. For example, using a handsome freestanding cabinet for extra storage or to serve as a standalone pantry. Any luxury elements in a busy family kitchen have to be durable. But beyond that, the options are nearly endless.

Of course, you may be lucky enough to have a huge kitchen and a budget to match. If that's the case, you'll be able to design different areas for particular functions—a wine bar, a spacious dining area, a professional-quality food-prep and cooking center —and use luxury features throughout. Whatever size your kitchen may be, one thing holds true: there are simply too many great design options to ever sacrifice style to function.

◀ **GO SPLASHY IN SMALL SPACES.** You can spend a little more where there is less area to cover—such as the solid surface, tiered quartz countertop and top-of-the-line stainless steel appliances used in this galley kitchen. The counter material is stronger than granite and every bit as handsome. Designer stools and spectacular hanging light fixtures round out a look that is the very height of small-space sophistication.

EXPLOIT THE WORK TRIANGLE. The triangle formed between the stove, sink/prep area, and refrigerator is the core of how efficient your kitchen will be. Experts call this the work triangle, and it should be as compact as possible to limit the number of steps you need to take from one area to the next. This compact kitchen includes an island sink that makes moving from food prep to cooktop as simple as turning around. Thoughtful layout like this is the key to any successful kitchen design, but is especially important in smaller rooms.

▲ **ADAPT TO NARROW KITCHENS.** Small, narrow kitchens require creativity to make the most of the limited space. The cabinets and countertops in this tiny room are narrower than standard, to allow for as much open floor space as possible. The stove, refrigerator, and sink are perfectly positioned in relationship to one another to ensure economy of movement in the room. Glass cabinet fronts make it easy to find exactly what you're looking for.

▲ **USE CLUTTER FOR COMFORT IN A SMALL KITCHEN.** As this kitchen layout shows, a small space doesn't necessarily need to be austere to be usable and welcoming. This cozy room uses a mix of open, vertical, and overhead storage to optimize every square inch. Although the kitchen appears to be jam packed, everything has a place, and it's easy to find whatever the cook might need. It's also a very homey look that seems both fun and comfortable.

▶ **LEVERAGE LIGHT TONES TO OPEN UP A SMALL KITCHEN.** The lovely natural wood finish and simple lines of the wall and base cabinets, along with the timeless muted green of the island, help visually expand this modest kitchen. The same idea drove the choice of light pine for the flooring rather than darker oak or other wood, and bright white for the ceiling. It helps that the window has not been blocked by a window treatment and that the countertop surfaces are all light and bright as well.

SMALL KITCHEN DESIGN TIPS AND TRICKS

Make your modest kitchen work harder and look better by leveraging strategies straight out of an interior designer's playbook.

• **GET MOBILE.** Rolling islands and cabinetry provide the most flexibility where space is tight. Wheels allow you to store a work surface or extra storage off to the side of the room until needed.

• **BE SHELF-ISH.** Exploit even small areas of bare wall with shelves sized to fit. Even a shallow spice shelf can alleviate some of the storage burden on cabinets in a small kitchen.

• **RACK IT.** Hanging storage—whether it's overhead pot racks or wall-mounted bar hangers—can be a great way to free up space in drawers and cabinets. The cookware and utensils you'd most likely hang tend to be space hogs and an inefficient use of enclosed storage.

• **MIRROR, MIRROR.** Mirrored surfaces will make the space seem larger and will bounce light around so that cramped counters are better illuminated for work tasks. You can mirror cabinet fronts, backsplashes, and even entire walls.

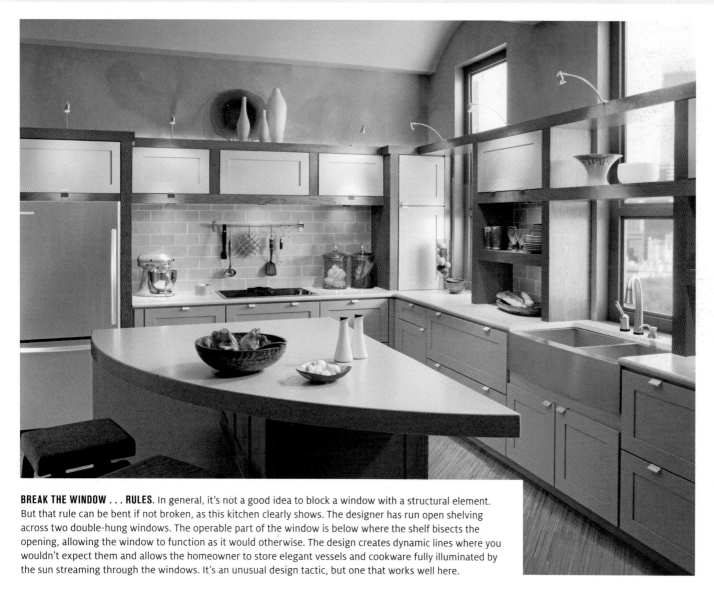

BREAK THE WINDOW . . . RULES. In general, it's not a good idea to block a window with a structural element. But that rule can be bent if not broken, as this kitchen clearly shows. The designer has run open shelving across two double-hung windows. The operable part of the window is below where the shelf bisects the opening, allowing the window to function as it would otherwise. The design creates dynamic lines where you wouldn't expect them and allows the homeowner to store elegant vessels and cookware fully illuminated by the sun streaming through the windows. It's an unusual design tactic, but one that works well here.

▲ **INTRODUCE DURABLE LUXURY INTO BUSY FAMILY KITCHENS.** The ebony floors here not only add a stunning design feature to this modest kitchen, they also hide dirt between cleanings, and the wood surface holds up well to heavy foot traffic in the space. Double gooseneck faucets and simple but elegant cabinet fronts provide style with eminently cleanable surfaces.

▶ **FOCUS ON THE FAUCET IN A FAMILY KITCHEN.** Inevitably, there were will be a lot of dishes and cookware to clean in any busy kitchen used by four or more family members (and the inevitable friends). A pro-quality faucet like the one show here—which can be detached from the mounting bracket to reach inside even deep pots—can make life noticeably easier and help keep a high-traffic room cleaner and more pleasant to use.

▲ **EXPAND THE NOTION OF ISLANDS IN A FAMILY KITCHEN.** A kitchen island can be many things. In this well-arranged kitchen, the extended island not only hosts the induction cooktop, it also stands in for a more traditional kitchen table. Handsome maple base cabinets match the cabinets used in the rest of the kitchen, effectively tying the look of this peninsula island to the kitchen as a whole. The light finish of the cabinets balances the effect of the nearly black floor and other gray elements, to create a look that's greater than the sum of its parts.

◄ **MAINTAIN VISUAL BALANCE TO CREATE A COMFORTABLE FAMILY KITCHEN.** Here, white granite countertops contrast the ebony cabinets to create striking eye candy. The light, neutral-colored mosaic tiles split the difference between the two extremes. This kitchen also features cost-cutting luxury in countertops that are not solid granite, but a granite shell made from the leftover scraps of solid countertop production. There's really no way to tell the difference except when you pay the bill.

▲ **BLEND FINISHES TO CREATE DYNAMIC VISUAL APPEAL IN A MIDSIZED KITCHEN.** Although the tendency of most homeowners is to use sedate, matching finishes on different surfaces and fixtures, you can create an exciting look by combining finishes. The brushed copper of the detailed country sink and pot-filler faucets is an eye-catching contrast to the bright white tile and sink. The natural wood counters and shelves jump out against the neutral tones and simple lines of the cabinets. The whole look holds together because neutral colors are used on the largest surfaces, forming a calming backdrop for the design.

▶ **KEEP THINGS OPEN AND AIRY TO MAKE A MEDIUM-SIZE KITCHEN LOOK LARGER.** The freestanding base cabinets in this kitchen, coupled with the light colors used throughout, glass-fronted wall-mount cabinets, and an open floor plan, create a more spacious feel to the kitchen and give it a fresh aspect. Freestanding cabinets can open up any kitchen, although the look is less formal than other types of cabinetry.

◀ **CENTER ISLANDS MAKE FOR EFFICIENT KITCHENS.** Using an island as the center of a busy family kitchen is a traditional layout technique that still works quite well. This island follows all the rules, being small enough to leave plenty of room for travel around the structure and big enough to serve multiple purposes—such as breakfast bar, prep surface, and open storage. It's also in keeping with the style of the kitchen.

◀ **DESIGN AHEAD FOR EASY CLEANUP.** Cleanable surfaces are key to keeping a busy mid-size kitchen looking its best at all times, with a minimum of effort. The square-edge solid surface countertops, glass tile backsplash, flat-front base cabinets, and glass-fronted wall-mount cabinets are all easy to clean with a quick swipe. The sharp contemporary lines of all the kitchen's features ensure that there are no nooks and crannies in which dirt can hide.

▶ **MAKE A MODEST KITCHEN SEEM OPULENT WITH SPECIAL FIXTURES AND SURFACES.** This modern kitchen isn't large but plays visually big thanks to a wealth of stunning, natural wood surfaces and sophisticated lighting that includes recessed ceiling lights, cabinet lighting, accent lights, and decorative lighting around the edge of the island countertop. The effect is one of super sophistication and polish and makes a big impact in a less-than-huge space.

▲ **ADD STYLE AND FUNCTION WITH CAREFULLY CHOSEN SPECIALTY FIXTURES.** Fixtures such as the pot-filler faucet shown here are not essential to a kitchen, but make a busy family kitchen much more efficient. Incorporating a countertop-mount style ensures that the faucet is as good at drawing attention as it is at making pasta prep a quicker chore. Whenever you're thinking about a pot-filler faucet, make sure that there is plenty of clearance all around so the function of the faucet is never blocked.

▲ **DISGUISE UTILITY FEATURES IN MEDIUM-SIZE KITCHENS.** This trash compacter has been concealed behind a faux cabinet front that matches the base cabinets in the room. Although a stainless steel front would have been a more conventional treatment, there's nothing pretty about a trash compactor and hiding it makes a lot of design sense. Notice how the illusion is made convincing by the addition of a drawer handle and pull.

ADD STYLE AND STORAGE WITH DISTINCTIVE POT RACKS. The straight-bar unit shown here is rugged and well suited to a busy family kitchen and country or contemporary design. This fixture, like most pot racks, adds a handsome, eye-catching feature that reinforces the notion of the kitchen as workspace and provides a wealth of storage for large, unwieldy pots and pans. The best thing about pot racks like this is that you can position them right over workspaces, so your cookware is at your fingertips any time you cook.

▲ **SELECT FLAT-FRONT CABINETS FOR A SLEEK LOOK THAT NATURALLY BLENDS WITH A LARGE KITCHEN SPACE.** Handleless cabinets like the upper cabinets in this kitchen provide an elegant visual flow in a large space. The unadorned cabinet doors add to a calm that complements the space and gives it a sophisticated feel. The cabinets also serve as the perfect foil for a dynamite black tile floor and display cabinets full of glassware.

▶ **CENTRALIZE THE WORK SURFACE IN A LARGE KITCHEN.** The long, large island in this warm and well-appointed kitchen not only hosts the induction cooktop, it also provides abundant prep area that can be accessed from all sides. It leaves plenty of room for multiple cooks to comfortably work in the same space. The island boasts a wealth of cabinetry that matches the surrounding wall and base units, and the look is both striking and informal.

▲ **ACCENT A LARGE KITCHEN WITH SPECIAL FEATURES THAT MIGHT NOT FIT IN A SMALLER SPACE.** The standout modern pendant chandeliers and the partially coffered ceiling in this room could overwhelm a more modest space. But in this kitchen, those features play stunningly against a background of contemporary cabinetry and modern ebonized flooring. It's a one-of-kind look made effective by the sheer size of the kitchen.

◄ **LET WHITE DOMINATE AN AMPLE KITCHEN.** Simple is sometimes best, and white used as the dominant hue in a large kitchen creates a stunningly clean look that emphasizes the expanse of the room. In tandem with the light-filled windows, the white cabinets in this kitchen create an airy, expansive feel. That vibe makes creating meals here a joy and makes this one of the most desirable and popular rooms in the house.

▲ **PLANK A LARGE KITCHEN AREA.** Plank flooring looks natural over the large expanse of a large kitchen's footprint. A wood appearance adds distinction to the space . . . but this floor isn't wood. It's an amazingly convincing laminate surface that can be a wonderful alternative to real wood flooring when the square footage you're covering is significant. Despite the high-end look, laminate is easier to install than wood, less expensive, durable, and easy to clean. The wide format maintains the expansive feel of the space.

◄ **ACCENT A LARGE KITCHEN WITH ELEGANT DETAILS.** Something as simple as a sophisticated countertop edge profile can have a big design impact. The tiered, ogee-style profile shown here is an eye-catching feature that helps define the space at large. The recycled-glass countertop adds just as much fascination to the room. Details like this help make a large kitchen really special, becoming something much more than just a great big space in which to cook and eat.

◄ **GIVE FINE CABINETRY THE STAGE IT DESERVES.**
Fine cabinet detailing is a sign of luxury,
especially elegant touches like the inner edge
profiles of these classic cabinets. Exquisite
details like the fluting, cornices, and dentil
molding on the wall-mounted cabinets can be
too busy and may overwhelm smaller kitchens.
But used in a substantial space like this, they
all combine to create a sophisticated classic
look that does the oversized kitchen justice.

▼ **ADD LUXURY TO A LARGE KITCHEN WITH
HIGH-END EQUIPMENT.** A restaurant-quality
addition like this six-burner gas range not only
brings a whole lot of cooking power to your
meal preparation, it adds bling to the room
and basically shouts that some serious eats
are going to be whipped up. And although it's
the poor craftsperson who blames their tools,
deluxe appliances such as these can sometimes
even spur more cooking and entertaining
adventures and make a gourmet out of a
weeknight cook.

STORE IN PLAIN SIGHT TO ADD LIFE. The large visual space in a luxury kitchen can sometimes lead to a cold "empty" feel, but not if you use exposed storage. Add features such as the wall-mounted shelves, sleek hanging rods, and rolling island caddy in this kitchen, and you provide delight for the eye. The dishes, cookware, and utensils all become graphic elements in their own right. But more to the point, they add a very human scale to the large space.

▲ **DEFINE LARGE SPACES WITH SIGNATURE CABINETRY.** In a sizeable kitchen, cabinets tend to be the most visible design element and subsequently have a huge impact on the overall look. The inset-panel framed units in this kitchen create a clean yet traditional aesthetic— not overly fussy nor coldly modern. The cabinets set the tone, and the wall color, shelves, flooring, and even the appliances are meant to complement them.

◀ **LEAVE OPEN SPACE WHERE A LARGE FOOTPRINT ALLOWS FOR IT.** It's natural to want to fill a large kitchen with an oversized island, extra storage cabinets and cupboards, and more. But sometimes, leaving space for movement and visual relief is the wiser design and functional solution. This kitchen is the perfect example of how blank space can benefit a large room. The stunning wood floor provides an attention-drawing focal point. The perimeter of the room is stocked with all the storage the owners could need, and a simple stainless steel island serves as an informal food prep and eating surface. The room is stylish, calming, and efficient.

ORDER A DESIGNED SPACE FOR AN UPSCALE LARGE KITCHEN WITH PROFESSIONAL POLISH. This entire kitchen—including cabinets, shelves, and work surfaces—was designed and manufactured by a single design company. The look is completely unified, and completely high fashion, with elm wood used throughout, in addition to marble surfaces. If you're willing to pay a premium, you can take all the guesswork out of your kitchen design or redesign.

MAKE EXTRA PREP SPACE WHEN YOU HAVE THE ROOM. Large kitchens can handle a lot of activity, but a good amount of that action will require prep work. The plumbed L that holds the sink in this kitchen adds an amazing amount of prep space to the handsome counter under the window. The appliances are all part of a suite, and each is strategically located where it makes the most sense for cooking and cleanup. It's a well-thought-out space that is a pleasure to use.

◀ **PLAY THE ANGLES IN A LARGE KITCHEN.** The bigger the kitchen floor plan, the better the chance you'll have odd shapes creep in. Here, a clipped corner presented a design challenge. The kitchen designer answered that challenge with corner cabinetry and a custom island angled to match the corner. Although they can represent significant design and layout challenges, corners can also be a chance to create dynamic visual interest in the space—as long you don't interfere with traffic flow.

▼ **MIX SHAPES IN A LARGE SPACE TO MAKE MODERN SPECIAL.** A linear modern kitchen design like this can start to appear a little severe without some visual relief from all the geometry. Curved shapes such as the round openings in the wine holder and the gooseneck faucet bring a bit of elegance to the room. But the stunning glass pendants with their sexy flowing lines and gleam serve as the ultimate counterpoint to the straight lines that dominate the kitchen design.

SCINTILLATING KITCHEN STYLES

Contemporary

Traditional

Modern

Country, Farmhouse & Cottage

There's nothing to stop you from creating your own unique kitchen design style. But there's a good chance you'll be reinventing the wheel. You could far more easily put your own spin on one of the many established kitchen design styles, by using signature elements alongside the key indicators of whatever style appeals to you. Manufacturers create cabinets, flooring, countertops, appliances, and accessories specifically to suit well-known styles, so much of the work will already be done for you. However, making any style your own requires knowing a little bit about what does—and does not—define it. The descriptions that follow describe the most popular kitchen design styles. There are many variations on any theme, but these are good starting points in choosing a look that suits your tastes and your particular kitchen space.

- **CONTEMPORARY.** Bridging the divide between traditional and modern, contemporary kitchens feature "clean," minimal aesthetics with a lack of curving lines, flowing shapes, fussy elements, or ornate fixtures. However, contemporary rooms generally include a few key traditional design elements that help warm the space up a bit. The style is also constantly evolving, because it is literally about the "now." So it can include design elements that are trending in the moment, such as the muted colors that are popular these days.

- **TRADITIONAL.** A more formal style, traditional kitchens are characterized by symmetry and elaborate details. Dark cherry or mahogany cabinets may feature fluting, rosettes, corbels, built-up door panels, and dentil crown molding. Countertops will often have compound edge profiles, and the room can include complicated backsplash tile patterns such as diamonds. The style is all about intricate, sumptuous surfaces and elaborate fixtures.

- **COUNTRY, FARMHOUSE, AND COTTAGE.** Turn to a country look for a more casual kitchen. This style is set apart by the use of simple, repetitive elements such as beadboard or faux beadboard cabinets and wall cladding.

▲ **ESTABLISH TRADITIONAL STYLE WITH RAISED-PANEL CABINETRY.** Although cabinets like the ones in this kitchen are a well-established look, they can be made fresh with eye-catching hardware. In this kitchen, a traditional gooseneck faucet includes modern convenience with a pull-down head, and a simple yet elegant glass oversink lighting fixture offers a bit of restrained style.

▲ **USE GLASS TO DEFINE CONTEMPORARY.** Glass surfaces are common to contemporary kitchens because they usually incorporate simple straight lines, unembellished edge profiles and a crisp, fresh look. The counters and wall tiles here bring a sparkle to the room that only glass can deliver. Frosted-glass-front cabinets add to the allure, and a new glass-front refrigerator carries through the theme in very cool fashion. Aside from the elegant and eye-catching look, glass surfaces make for quick and easy clean up.

▶ **CELEBRATE CONTEMPORARY WITH CLEAN LINES.** Sleek and elegant lines like the clean edge of this solid surface counter, the simple shape of the sink, and futuristic L-shape of the ultra-cool faucet in this kitchen all reinforce the notion of "contemporary." Subtle and beautiful wall tiles and high-end frameless cabinets in dark bamboo add a bit of life and warmth to the room, softening the unyielding aspect of the crisp, uncomplicated lines.

ECO-FRIENDLY KITCHEN DESIGN

Whether you're doing a floor-to-ceiling kitchen remodel, or just tackling a modest update, you can build in environmentally responsible elements that will be good for the planet and great for your pocketbook.

- **LIGHTING.** Replace incandescent bulbs with compact fluorescents (CFLs) or LED bulbs. Although these may be pricier than the incandescent bulbs, they will also last a lot longer and use far less energy. All that usually makes them a better value in the long run.

- **FLOORING (AND CUTTING BOARDS, BACKSPLASHES, ETC.).** Bamboo and cork are renewable flooring and wall surface options. It doesn't hurt that both are offered in a range of eye-catching appearances, and the prices for these "green" options continue to fall.

- **COUNTERTOPS.** Recycling is all the rage in kitchen countertops. You can find fascinating recycled stone-chip and composite countertops in looks that mimic granite and marble. Or turn to the many recycled-glass countertops for a unique look in a color that suits the rest of the room. You can even find recycled-paper counters that have been treated to be water and scratch resistant.

- **APPLIANCES.** Always look for the Energy Star rating label on new appliances. The label spells out how much energy the unit you're looking at will use relative to other models. Find the most energy-efficient refrigerator or electric stove you can buy, and you'll be saving a significant amount on the home energy bill every month.

▲ **CREATE CONTEMPORARY EXCITEMENT WITH A VARIETY OF SHAPES AND SIZES.** Although contemporary style is, by its nature, restrained, a mix of shapes and textures is a way to spice up the look. The ribbed-glass cabinet fronts, oblong lighting fixtures, glass-tiled backsplash, and the two-tiered, two-toned, solid-surface countertop all add an enviable measure of visual interest to what could have been a neutral-colored, overly low-key space.

▲ **DISTINGUISH A CONTEMPORARY KITCHEN WITH DISTINCTIVE FLOORING.** But that flooring also needs to be durable, long-lasting, and cleanable. The vinyl plank product used in this kitchen fits the bill on all counts. The look is similar to stone, but at a much lower cost, in a flooring that is easier to install. The color provides a wonderful counterpoint to the other tones in the kitchen, without straying from the contemporary style.

▲ **REINFORCE CONTEMPORARY STYLE WITH STAINLESS STEEL.** The clean, sharp appearance and lack of color or pattern make stainless steel a perfect surface material for just about any contemporary kitchen. The dual wall-mounted stoves, island counter, bullet pendant lights, and sink backsplash in this kitchen not only provide a sleek complement to the bamboo cabinets, they also lead the eye through the kitchen's design.

◄ **CREATE MYSTERY WITH FROSTED GLASS.** Frosted-glass cabinet inserts achieve two kitchen design goals: they brighten the look with a sophisticated cabinet element, and they conceal what's inside, so that you don't have to worry about the artfulness of what you put in your cabinets. Frosted glass is also an ideal look for the minimal, sleek nature of a contemporary kitchen, and the material is on par with the cost of plain glass inserts.

▲ **LET CABINETS DEFINE THE ROOM.** A great way to establish a style for your kitchen is by starting with the cabinets—the choice of which will drive other choices. Here, high-quality cherry cabinets set the stage for solid surface countertops and unique metal tiles with a relief surface design. The light tone of the cabinets provides relief for the eye and ties all the other elements together. Given the range of cabinet styles—from ready-to-assemble unadorned units to totally over-the-top custom cabinets—it's easy to find exactly the look you want and build the rest of the design from there.

▶ **GO LINEAR TO EXPLOIT CONTEMPORARY STYLE.** The open, floating shelves in this kitchen are the height of simplicity and they provide ample space for displaying attractive plates, glasses, and cookware. They also carry through a theme thick with lines, one that is echoed in the shape of the high-end range and the stunning patterns of the glass tile on the wall. Lines are an easy design point to build on in a contemporary kitchen.

▼ **SOFTEN A CONTEMPORARY LOOK WITH THE APPEAL OF EXOTIC WOOD.** The wood plank floor in this sleek, appealing kitchen is complemented by stunning cabinets faced with tigerwood veneer. The flowing lines of the graining, along with elements such as the brushed nickel gooseneck faucet, help relieve the abundance of straight lines in the kitchen. The overall appearance becomes warm and welcoming.

▲ **GO SCANDINAVIAN WITH PLAIN WHITE CABINETS.** A popular version of contemporary style is the clean look of frameless white cabinets with simple handles, against a neutral background. The look is made somewhat more dramatic with a gray slate floor that isn't really gray slate—it's durable, cleanable vinyl sheet. The subtleties in the surface pattern of this floor provide visual relief in what might otherwise have been an overly stark kitchen.

▶ **SIMPLIFY FIXTURES TO SUIT A CONTEMPORARY DESIGN.** In any contemporary kitchen, fixtures are accents that can play against or with the overall design itself. Simpler versions, such as the handsome and functional faucet and stainless-steel sink in this kitchen (the head pulls out for use as a sprayer), do the look justice without calling too much attention to themselves. The chrome faucet finish is an appealing and popular choice for use in contemporary settings.

◄ **LEVERAGE CONTRAST.** Part of what separates contemporary from modern and traditional kitchens is the use of clearly contrasting design elements to create a bit of visual tension. Here, the ornate backsplash tile pattern plays against the strong simple straight lines in the cabinetry. The engineered stone surface of the island countertop contrasts the warm wood floor and the soft upholstered chairs. It's a look that maintains visual interest without overwhelming the design with busy details.

▼ **SPRUCE UP A NEUTRAL SCHEME BY MIXING LIGHTS AND DARKS.** Although this kitchen doesn't feature a lot of bold or dynamic colors, it still features a ton of visual interest thanks to a mix of light and dark tones. Dark brown cabinets are offset by a tan wall tile and light wood island, while beige flooring and gray walls provide a soothing backdrop to all the other decorative elements. It's the perfect balance of low-key hues and contrast.

PANTRY STRATEGIES

It doesn't matter if your pantry is a full room off the kitchen, a large standing closet, or even just a few cupboards. Instituting a few effective strategies will keep the space more organized, make it look nicer, and make it a whole lot easier to get to the staples you need when cooking.

• **LABEL, LABEL, LABEL.** The problem with many pantries is that they become repositories for foodstuffs that are not regularly used. This inevitably leads to clutter from out-of-date staples that are well past their prime. A big, visible label stuck on boxes, bags, jars, and other containers can provide at-a-glance convenience so you can rotate stock when necessary. Neatly print the date purchased, the date of expiration, and any other relevant information.

• **USE THE DOORS.** Plain pantry cupboard or cabinet doors are nice enough, but they are also valuable organizational real estate. Paint the front of a pantry cupboard with blackboard paint as an easy way to keep track of the weekly shopping list. Line the inside of the doors with corkboard to pin up coupons, recipes, and more. Or hang one of the many wire organizers on the inside of pantry doors to keep small items such as spice jars organized and ready for use.

• **DE-BAG.** Bags are imperfect containers in a pantry. Some, such as bags of flour, are prone to leaking. Others, such as bags of bulk-item purchases, are loose forms that take up more space than they need. That's why it's wise to transfer bulk or bagged purchases into more standardized containers, such as sealed glass jars or plastic buckets (don't forget the labels!).

• **STAIRSTEP.** Different size cans and jars present a challenge on pantry shelves. It's just too easy for a small container to be hidden in the back, behind large cans and bottles. The answer? Stairstep shelving. This type of organizer is inexpensive and ingenious, and lets you see exactly what you're keeping on a pantry shelf at a glance.

• **ACCOMMODATE COOKWARE.** We think of pantries as places just for food. But if you have extra room, your panty can be a great place to organize baking sheets, muffin tins, and cake pans. A high and deep shelf can become the ideal bakeware or cookware storage with the help of a few aftermarket horizontal dividers. A sturdy shelf can be the preferred location for a row of enameled cast-iron pots and pans.

▶ **DO DARK AND DRAMATIC TO MAKE A TRADITIONAL STATEMENT.** It's not just the frames and raised panels that make these cabinets traditional—it's the deep, rich stain. A dark wood look is widely associated with traditional style, and the owner of this kitchen has pepped up the look with a wonderful wine rack wall and matching glass-front cabinets (all purchased as a suite from the same manufacturer). The truth is, finishes can determine style every bit as much as form can.

▲ **CHOOSE APPLIANCES TO BALANCE THE LOOK.** Although many people think appliances should simply fade into the background, the beauty of modern appliances makes them perfect for display. Here, a stainless steel wall-mount oven counteracts the visually heavy feel of a dark run of cabinets, and a deep gray backsplash and countertop. The finish of the appliance actually blends with the finish of the cabinet pulls and handles, and the appearance is made more stunning with the use of the stainless steel front.

▲ ◄ **DRESS UP A TRADITIONAL KITCHEN WITH A TRULY DISTINCTIVE PERIOD FAUCET.** This highly detailed fixture is a perfect example of the type of beautiful options offered by today's faucet manufacturers. Not only is the faucet designed to mimic a traditional farmhouse style, but the silver finish is utterly alluring. For a modest design element, it adds immeasurably to the kitchen.

◄ **USE STANDOUT TILE TO BRING EXCITEMENT TO THE TRADITIONAL KITCHEN.** A marble tile backsplash in a fascinating diamond pattern (lit up with the help of undercabinet lighting) complements white counters and provides a lot of zing against the sedate backdrop of gray cabinetry. Although solid colors are a common trait in traditional kitchen designs, a sophisticated pattern such as this—and the undeniably luxurious material—definitely has a place in the style.

▲ SERVE A TRADITIONAL KITCHEN WITH APPROPRIATE LIGHTING FIXTURES. Lighting can be an afterthought in any kitchen, but poorly chosen fixtures are exceptionally jarring in an identifiable style such as traditional. Here, drum pendants maintain the identity and meld perfectly with the rest of the elements in the kitchen, while providing fascinating visuals in their own right. Notice the matching sconce used near the sink—repetitive fixture styles are a great way to lead the eye through a kitchen's design, regardless of style.

▶ EXPLOIT CURVES AND FACADES. Flowing shapes and facings for common features such as refrigerators, other appliances, and the hood covering in this kitchen are hallmarks of traditional style. Notice how the façade over the range hood matches the finish and detailing on the cabinets throughout the space, and how the shape of the faucet mimics the window's arches. It's a design full of elegance in motion.

◀ **HIDE YOUR HOOD.** Stainless steel doesn't fit comfortably into some traditional room designs and the answer is a hood overlay like the one shown here. It's an elegant solution where you want a somewhat warmer feel than cold steel. Both cabinet and appliance manufacturers are increasingly offering these kinds of overlays as luxury upgrades. You can find them to match just about any finish, or paintable so that you can customize to suit your particular design.

▲ **DETAILS FOCUS ON THE TRADITIONAL.** Fluted columns, corbels, and frieze-ornamented cornices all make this a special kitchen and announce a traditional style. The visually stunning detailing of the cabinets and shelves is matched by their elegant muted green color. The fluted apron-front sink follows through on the theme, and the subway tile used for the backsplashes is the perfect decorative touch to contrast all the other flourishes in this room's design.

CAP THE DESIGN WITH CABINETS. Cabinetry is extremely important in defining a traditional style kitchen, and the cabinets usually set the tone for the rest of the decorative elements. But you can choose cabinets to accessorize as well, such as these beautiful units with glass-fronted top cabinets. The diamond muntins and tiered cornice scream high style without going over the top or outside the realm of what makes traditional traditional.

▲ **MAKE SURE THE SMALL DETAILS MATCH THE KITCHEN STYLE.** The ogee profile on the edge of the stunning quartz counter in this traditional Cape Cod–style kitchen is true to the look. But it also adds a bit of polish to the otherwise basic lines and finishes in the space. Modest details like this can be powerful finishing touches to any design, indicating professional designer influences.

◀ **FINISH TO MATCH YOUR STYLE.** Certain wood finishes are associated with the traditional kitchen style. These include the cherry finish shown here, mahogany stains, and dark walnut. Ebony stains, however, risk losing the fine details in cabinet profiles, columns, and corbels that are also so much a part of the traditional look. That's also why the finish is usually satin or semigloss for this style's cabinets.

▲ **MAKE MODERN INTRIGUING BY CONCEALING *AND* REVEALING.**
The open and hidden areas of storage in this modern kitchen
provide a measure of visual intrigue in an otherwise spare
space. Modern kitchens risk looking sterile, but having
cookware and dishes on display adds warmth to the look. Not
to mention, this strategy makes these items more accessible.
The wood trim on the cabinets also adds a bit of relief in the
largely monochromatic room.

▶ **GO FAUX FOR SAVINGS.** Modern can be an expensive
kitchen style to put in place, but you can get around some of
the expense by using convincing and durable faux materials.
Although this sleek, thick counter looks every bit as much
stainless steel as the high-tech range hood, it is in fact,
laminate. Modern laminates can be found mimicking all kinds
of metals, stones, and even wood, and they are both durable
and easy to work with.

ACCESSORIZE FOR MOD. Sleek sinks are a way to bring flair to a modern kitchen, and a round sink is unusual in any setting. This fashionable faucet-and-sink combo is a space-saving island addition and simple design feature that still brings a lot of visual impact. Sinks and faucets are fairly inexpensive ways to think out of the box and incorporate a slightly different look in your kitchen design.

SMALL DETAILS SPEAK LOUDLY IN MODERN DESIGN. Because modern kitchen design is defined by Spartan spaces, and clean, uncluttered lines and angles, little touches like the fine design handles shown here can play much larger than they normally would. There are a wealth of interesting handles and pulls on the market and it's easy to find a style that is both modern and to your taste.

DON'T FORGET THE HOOD STYLE. Cooktop hoods can often be afterthoughts in kitchen design, but a multi-feature, high-end hood such as the one shown here can accent a modern kitchen in fine style. This hood features multiple speeds, a digital readout, and integrated work lights, all in a cool linear package that would be at home in any modern setting. Hood manufacturers make many models to fit a modern setting.

▲ **GO BOLD.** Although modern kitchen design is most often associated with bright white or neutral surfaces, you can bring your own signature to a modern kitchen with the judicious use of color. The kitchen here maintains a modern aesthetic with its sharp lines and angles and uncluttered décor. But it also leverages the power of color in the frameless cabinetry and the stunning recycled-glass countertop. Both feature high-tech materials—another signature of modern style.

▶ **BRIGHT EQUALS MODERN.** Much as modern is associated with clean, crisp lines, it's also defined by sharp, bright white lights. The halogens and LED fixtures used in this kitchen produce crisp white light perfect for a room that needs to be clean and easy to work in. Undercounter lights emphasize the stunning quartz countertops, while undercabinet lighting ensures that the surfaces are safe and easy to use.

MAGNIFY A MODERN SPACE WITH EDGY LIGHTING FIXTURES. Modern style is accommodating of design elements that might be too far out for any other kitchen design. The space-age lighting fixtures in this kitchen and matching dining area perfectly complement the style of room. But they also stand out as design features on their own, drawing the eye back and forth between the kitchen and dining area.

MATCH MODERN TO THE SPACE. A galley kitchen in a loft calls for an adapted modern design that better suits the space. The designer of this kitchen included the sharp stainless steel appliances you would expect, but incorporated subtly colored and textured cabinets that you wouldn't. The modern vibe is kept alive in the space with a white solid-surface countertop and a chrome X-leg dining table, but the look is as unique as it is modern.

CONSIDER A MODERN BLANK SLATE. Stay true to the uncluttered, linear perspective that defines modern style, and you can riff on it at the margins. Here, small points of color are captured in shelves and the drum shades of hanging light fixtures. The room is warmed up with wood tones and a simple band of glass tiles. A black range hood matches the black appliances used in the space and reinforces the modern aesthetic with a futuristic flair.

◄ **MAKE MODERN ACCESSIBLE WITH PATTERNS.** Although pure white counter surfaces would have been more predictable in this kitchen, they also may have been far too sterile. Instead, the homeowner went with stunning quartz surfaces with a painterly surface pattern in browns and beiges that complement the other tones in the room. The counters set up appealing visual tension between the free-flowing patterns and the more regimented appearances of the other materials in the kitchen.

▼ **STORE ITEMS IN PLAIN SIGHT TO ADD LIFE TO A STEREOTYPICAL MODERN DESIGN.** Crisp lines, minimal color, and hard reflective surfaces give this kitchen a thoroughly modern look. But containers, vases, serving ware, and more—stored on shelves, in open cupboards, and on top of cabinets—provide relief from what could be a very stern look. The different items also introduce splashes of color and pattern that make the room more interesting, while never undercutting its modern cred.

▲ **MODERNIZE FAUCETS JUST LIKE THE REST OF THE KITCHEN.**
Faucets are naturally a way to add intriguing curvy forms to
an otherwise linear design style, but that doesn't mean you
should pick the first chrome gooseneck you come across.
The faucets in any modern setting are a chance to make a
statement, as the twin units in this kitchen do. With painted
bodies and heads, the faucets are simple, but stand out. The
beautiful form is only made more intriguing by the two-tone
look, and the units work every bit as well they look.

▶ **STICK WITH STAINLESS STEEL TO STAY TRUE TO A
MODERN DESIGN.** The suite of appliances in this kitchen,
including separate single-door refrigerator and freezer,
don't call attention to themselves, but the steel surfaces
are sleek enough to fit nicely with the modern cabinets
and marble floor. Although it's popular to clad the front
of large appliances in surfaces matching surrounding
cabinets, that look is more applicable to a contemporary
or traditional kitchen.

▶ **DEFY CONVENTION.** The designer of this kitchen decided against wall-mounted cabinets, creating even more of an open feel to the room. The choice is inspired, because it reinforces the clean look that marks modern designs. That look is also helped by the rugged concrete countertops and the sophisticated—and super eco-friendly—marmoleum click flooring. The sum of the parts is a complete look that shouts "modern."

▲ **TILE A BACKSPLASH FOR VISUAL RELIEF.** A tiled backsplash can have an effect far beyond its modest size. The cooktop backsplash in this small modern kitchen adds a whole lot of visual interest with the rectangular grid work and lovely blue color. The tile complements the other monochromatic and linear elements in the room, but also stands out as an elegant focal point in the spare, stylish space.

OPT FOR RAW IN INDUSTRIAL MODERN. This room is full of rough-hewn life with the plywood vertical island surfaces and concrete floors. The exposed edges of the countertop and shelves appears to be plywood as well, but is actually a sophisticated laminate surface, modern, edgy, and beautiful. The frosted-glass cabinet doors provide a simple, sophisticated, and subtle backdrop to what is a fairly dramatic modern island.

▶ COLOR COUNTRY KITCHENS IN CLASSIC TONES. The yellow here is right out of history and creates the perfect backdrop for stunning blue counters, antique-reproduction ceiling fixtures, and a fireclay farmhouse apron-front sink. The cabinets come equipped with detailing to match the historic paint and help create a beautiful and memorable kitchen design that is pure old-timey charm.

▼ TAKE COUNTRY FROM ARCHITECTURAL CUES. The A-frame, exposed beam-and-rafter construction of this kitchen is reminiscent of a barn or farmhouse, so the designer filled the oversized space with country kitchen design elements, such as the simple recessed panel cabinets, wicker basket storage, and hanging fixtures that are reminiscent of candle lanterns. Decorative dinnerware on display adds to the effect. Country kitchen design is often thought of as a small room aesthetic, but here it works on a grand scale.

BRING FARMHOUSE STYLE TO LIFE WITH SUBTLY DETAILED CABINETRY. Although the cabinets in this kitchen look simple, the detailing is actually a thoughtfully accurate updated representation of authentic farmhouse cabinets. The recessed panels are true to the style, and arching kick plates create faux legs as if the cabinets were freestanding. Beautifully simple handles drive the impression home, and a copper range hood with decorative relief is the icing on the cake.

SET THE STYLE WITH THE SINK. No sink is quite so distinctive as an apron-front "farmhouse" sink. Named for the formidable cast-iron fixtures that served as gigantic cleaning repositories for real farmhouses, this style of sink is beautiful and extremely useful because it is normally extremely deep. This particular version features an elegant tiered ledge and a stunning chrome faucet with white porcelain handles in keeping with the style of the sink. An incorporated soap holder makes the faucet even more useful.

TIPS

UTENSIL MANAGEMENT

Some of the most frequently used cooking instruments are some of the hardest to wrangle in the kitchen. Kitchen utensils can take up a lot of drawer space, and tend to be hard to find when you need them. But organizing them is a creative opportunity, and the first step is getting them out of the drawer.

• **JAR YOUR TOOLS.** Use decorative jars, mason jars, or even vases to segregate your utensils by type along a shelf or portion of a countertop. This is a great way to keep spatulas, whisks, and more ready for use and close to food prep areas.

• **HOLSTER YOUR FAVORITES.** If you tend to use the same utensils over and over again, park them in wall-mounted "holsters." These are nothing more than loops of leather or stiff fabric riveted, stapled, or screwed to a decorative painted board (which is itself fastened to a kitchen wall).

• **HOOK IT.** You'll find decorative hooks in just about every size, style, and material imaginable. Create a row of hooks to place utensils right where you want them and to use them as decorative elements in and of themselves. A variation on the hook theme, a hanging rail, is just as useful for storing utensils out in the open as it is for pans.

▷ **COUNTRIFY SMALL DETAILS.** The ring of truth in any distinctive style is often established with the small convincing details. This chunky latch serves in place of a standard handle and catch, and provides a realistic antique farmhouse look to the cabinets. Hooded pulls in an antique finish could do the same. Details like this can make or break a stylized kitchen design.

▲ **USE WOOD TO ANNOUNCE FARMHOUSE STYLE.** The wonderfully chunky wood island shown here, with its thick turned columns and matching wood-trimmed pot rack, sets the stage for the kitchen. The other cabinets follow suit, featuring a distressed finish, dish drying rack, and niche shelves—all indicators of country farmhouse style and all quaint design elements that create a lovely atmosphere in this kitchen. Keep in mind that the style is most closely associated with pine and oak, so if you're going to show a natural-finish wood surface in the space, best to use those.

CREATE A TUSCAN COUNTRY LOOK WITH STONE. The luxurious stone floor and diamond-pattern stone wall behind the range in this kitchen not only warm up the room, they also give it the feel of Italian countryside villa. These surfaces are indestructible and easy to clean as well. Antique reproduction ceiling pendants add to the feel, and a marble-topped wood island emphasizes the idea of lasting luxury. A chef-quality two-stove range with industrial hood fits right in with the rest of the design elements, mimicking the squat good looks of a wood-fired stove you might have found in an actual large Italian country house.

INDICATE COUNTRY STYLE WITH BEADBOARD. A design element that most definitely establishes old-fashioned kitchen design right out of a farm is a beadboard surface. The cabinets in this lovely, warm kitchen show the simple appeal of beadboard. They also boast antique-style pulls and handles, along with faux feet that really establish the impression of country style. Exposed beams drive the style home, as does the knotty pine flooring.

STORE IN PLAIN SIGHT IN A COUNTRY KITCHEN. The informal nature of country, farmhouse, or cottage-style kitchens means cookware, plates, glasses, and more are kept out on display. Open shelving often replaces cabinetry, and pot racks—like the handsome, rough-hewn version here—are a regular feature in the style. Set over the island, this rack not only adds a lot of visual interest, it also puts pots and pans right where they are needed.

GET FUNKY WITH COUNTRY. A country look lends itself to a little freestyle riffing on the theme. The designer here created the foundation of a country kitchen with the simple cabinets and diamond-pattern stone floor. But a leaded-glass window, subway tile wall, and detailed cornice over the refrigerator all embellish the look with slight departures from the theme. Luxury stainless steel appliances provide visual focal points around the room and help guide the eye through the design.

COLOR IN THE KITCHEN

White is a wonderful, natural choice for any kitchen. White shows even the slightest hint of dirt, making it easier to keep clean. White reflects light, ensuring that a space where illumination equals safety is always as bright as can be. And white goes with anything; it can complement any appliance color or finish.

On the flip side, too much white can seem dull, uninteresting, and even sterile and stark. Given that more and more manufacturers offer fixtures and accents in a range of colors, there's no reason you can't add your favorite hues into the mix. Inject a little (or a lot of) color into your kitchen design and you potentially add fun, visual interest, and put your own signature on the look. Of course, the more or bolder colors you add, the more chances you take that the look could go awry.

That's why it's always good to try out new colors in the kitchen with smaller accents and colored areas, expanding the use of color as you get a good idea of how any shade works in the space. Keep in mind that the perception of any given color isn't just about the color itself. A bright, glossy finish will make the underlying color seem lighter than it really is. A matte finish will do the opposite.

On the same note, colors can alter the perception of the space itself. Lighter, brighter colors generally make any space seem larger. Darker colors and matte surfaces have a tendency to make the room seem cozier and smaller. Any color on the red-orange-yellow side of the color wheel will make a kitchen feel physically warmer. Blues and greens will have the opposite effect.

All that makes colors practical as well as aesthetic elements in the kitchen. Start with colors that appeal to you and complement those you've used elsewhere in the house. Choose an area to color and a finish. With a little planning and thoughtfulness, you'll wind up with a stunning kitchen that delights the eye.

△ COMPLEMENT COLOR WITH DISTINCTIVE SINK FINISHES.
Manufacturers now offer sinks in different finishes, shades, and colors, including the exceptional matte black shown here. In this case, the sink becomes the perfect natural color complement to a muted-yellow countertop. An elegant arching chrome faucet with an easy-to-use handle and pull-down spray head makes this colorful picture as useful as it is visually delightful.

▷ CONTAIN COLOR WITH MATCHING FIXTURES. Ensuring that fixtures throughout the space are finished in the same material and sheen gives the eye places to pause when it's processing strong color. Here, a brushed stainless steel sink and elegant matching faucet moderate the effect of a bold red countertop. A white sink would have worked as well, but it would have been less easy to match it to a high-style white faucet. The sink's apron front is an unusual design element that adds shape to a colorful visual and holds its own against the fiery backdrop of the counter.

◁ BE FEARLESSLY BOLD WHEN YOU'RE SURE. If you absolutely love certain colors and you plan on owning your home for a good long time (if not the rest of your life), then don't be afraid to take the plunge and color the space to suit your preferences. This kitchen reflects just such a bold decision, indulging the homeowner's love of neon colors. The space is vibrant, high-energy, and happy. The color scheme is actually a coordinated complementary scheme with an analogous addition (the orange). It may not be for everyone, but it adds life and excitement to what might otherwise be a sedate space.

▲ **DOMINATE A WHITE, MODERN KITCHEN WITH A SINGLE COLOR USED IN CABINETS AND SHELVES.**
The teal of the storage areas in this kitchen pops against the bright white background, giving it even more oomph than it normally would have. Using a single strong color in this way is incredibly effective—although it works best in modern, contemporary, or eclectic settings. Pick the color carefully because it isn't cheap or easy to paint or order cabinets in a color such as this.

▶ **COMBINE COLOR AND TEXTURE FOR BIG, BIG BANG.** The only thing better than a truly sophisticated midrange blue tile is if that color sits underneath a randomly undulating surface. A backsplash or wall of tile like this can transform the kitchen, inviting the hands as well as the eyes, and creating a vivid focal point in the room. Use glass tile like this, and you'll also be incorporating an easy-to-clean surface that won't break the bank.

PARTNER PATTERN AND COLOR.
Whether it's an exotic form of marble, wildly painted tile, or a recycled-glass countertop like the one shown here, pattern is a natural companion to color, especially bold color. The color shows the variations in shapes and lines to its best advantage. A countertop like this can be a fairly risk-free way to introduce strong color into a kitchen, because if you limit it to one run of base cabinets, it can easily and inexpensively be replaced if you find the color is not exactly the one for you.

▷ **MARRY COLOR AND PATTERN FOR ULTIMATE FASCINATION.** This textured tile backsplash in vibrant green provides an incredible focal point for the kitchen sink area. The curvy motif is echoed in the dramatic design of the two-tone faucet, with a stunning asymmetrical shape. The deep green complements the black granite counter, and the choice of black and brushed stainless steel faucet body ensures that the fixture doesn't get lost against the busy background.

▽ **EASE INTO COLOR IN THE KITCHEN WITH MUTED TONES AND SINGLE WALL EXPOSURE.** The robin's-egg blue on the back wall of this kitchen blends perfectly not only with the blue mosaic tile behind the stove, but also with the pervasive white and off-white tones throughout the room. Small accents and art sprinkled about echo the color family, but no instance of color overpowers any other in the space. It's a light touch that isn't likely to grow dated.

▲ **GO GRAY FOR A SOPHISTICATED LOOK THAT WON'T GROW OLD.** Gray tones are generally compatible with the entire spectrum of other colors. Just check out color samples carefully because many grays carry strong undertones of other colors, such as blue or green. Buying colored cabinets and shelves like the elegant prefab units in this kitchen is a great way of ensuring the color is professional and beautiful.

▲ **PICK A CLASSIC COLOR COMBO FOR A TIMELESS KITCHEN LOOK.** Blue-and-white kitchens tend to look fresh long after the design is finished and installed. Bold, deep-blue cabinets in this kitchen pop when set against the white elements like the apron sink. Ornamenting the cabinets with finely detailed silver knobs and pulls is a finishing touch that brings class and sophistication to the colors, and adds immeasurably to what is already a stunningly colorful look.

THINK BEYOND STAINLESS STEEL FOR YOUR HIGH-END APPLIANCES. Several manufacturers have joined the color parade with limited palettes of elegant colors to front their ranges, fridges, ovens, and other appliances. The four examples shown here represent the lovely range of offerings. Because these are fairly expensive appliances, you should choose a color carefully. But find the right one, and it can be the focal center point of your kitchen. The manufacturers have also taken pains to ensure the painted surface is every bit as cleanable and durable as stainless steel is.

Special Section

CHILL WITH COLORS IN AN UNEXPECTED PLACE. Tinted refrigerators are a fairly new addition to the kitchen lineup, but can be a showstopper when used correctly. Some manufacturers offer completely colored versions, such as the incredibly fun and unusual jewel-toned units shown here. Others simply offer front panels that can be swapped in and out, to give the refrigerator a different look at different times. These are better used in traditional settings where the refrigerator is nested in a cavity and the sides don't show.

▲ **PLAY IT SAFE BY COLORING WITH TRADITION.** Certain classic colors are inextricably linked to a certain design style. Using these hues in the style for which they were intended is an easy way to liven up a space with color. The dusty cornflower blue used in this country kitchen is the ideal marriage of simple form and lines with a color that's completely associated with that particular style. A muted-cream yellow would have been just as appropriate, and just as timeless.

▶ **SYNC YOUR SINK COLORS.** One of the marvelous modern innovations among today's manufacturers is coordinated sink and faucet color sets. A neutral tone such as the light brown sugar color of this sink and faucet are a safe choice, but one that will still draw a lot of attention in the kitchen. Although you can choose one of these sets in a color that contrasts the countertop, a more timeless look is a complementary pairing like the one shown here.

BRING CALM WITH GREEN. Midrange and lighter greens are associated with nature, being the color of grass, leaves, and seedlings. Not surprising then that using splashes of green in the kitchen can create a feeling of calm in what can be a very hectic space. The secret is to stay away from overly bright greens that can seem a little too "neon" when covering a surface. This backsplash is an example of lovely and subtle midrange green, one that won't grow tired over time.

CONSIDER THE MATERIAL WHEN CONSIDERING A COLOR. Colors can read very differently on different materials. A fire-engine red like the one shown here could quickly look old if used on a matte surface in a kitchen. But as the coloring in a polished volcanic rock countertop, it brightens and comes to life. The surface treatment of this counter means that the color has incredible visual depth and richness, almost as if lit from within. If you love bold color, this is a great surface for it.

▶ **CREATE COLOR SURPRISES.** A root beer–brown sink that matches the finishes on base cabinets is a brilliant addition to this kitchen. Part of the charm is that the sink is concealed from view from many points in the kitchen. Only when the viewer approaches it, does its color become revealed. This use of color in the kitchen can be intriguing, engaging, and incredibly effective as a decorative device. The stylish chrome faucet adds a bit of brightness to the sink and complements it perfectly.

▶ **SEEK OUT UNUSUAL COLOR APPLICATIONS.** The edge profiles of these paper-based fiber composite countertops come in different color combinations. It's a small color element but interesting and eye-catching. It doesn't hurt that these countertops are eco-friendly recycled paper— incredibly durable and easy to work with.

▲ **ESCHEW GLOSS FOR A DIFFERENT LOOK. KITCHEN COLOR DOESN'T HAVE TO BE GLOSSY TO BE BEAUTIFUL.** It's easy to fall into the trap of thinking all color surfaces in the kitchen must be shiny color surfaces. A gloss surface can sometimes make the color underneath seem a bit garish, or visually read too bright. The backsplash here shows what can be achieved with a more understated matte or satin surface. Even though these are glass tiles, you wouldn't know it from the sophisticated complementary colors under a nonreflective surface. Fortunately, the tiles are just as easy to clean as their high-gloss cousins.

▲ **INTRODUCE COLOR IN FIXTURES.** This gold-toned faucet is just one in a slew of new finishes that faucet manufacturers—and other kitchen suppliers—are adding to their lines. It's not just faucets either. Light fixtures, cabinet hardware, and hooks and brackets are all a chance to add splashes of your favorite hues into your kitchen design scheme. It doesn't hurt that the faucets featuring distinctive colors and shades also offer elegant forms such as the one shown here, which includes a pull-down spray head and streamlined, easy-to-use handle.

◀ **CONFINE COLORS TO COUNTERTOPS TO KEEP FROM OVERWHELMING THE SPACE.** The light green of the countertops used in this modern kitchen gives the space a fresh feel and makes it appear less sterile than it would if it had been kept all white. However, limiting the color to the countertops balances the visual weight in the space and ensures that it still holds true to a modern design aesthetic.

SPECTACULAR SURFACES

Captivating Countertops
& Backsplashes

Fabulous Floors

Separating kitchen design from that of other rooms in the house is the fact that wall, floor, and counter surfaces are usually divided into discreet surface areas, based on the placement of cabinets, fixtures, appliances, and furnishings. Those separate areas represent design opportunities. A painted wall can give way to a tiled backsplash underneath cabinets. Counters along a wall may be one material, while the counter on an island or L is entirely different.

That variety is what makes designing or redesigning a kitchen so very exciting. Of course, the variety also presents challenges.

That's why, when choosing kitchen surfaces, it's best to start with the largest background surfaces (usually the walls, ceiling, and floor) and then select other surface materials based on what will work best with the larger areas. That's certainly not to say that you need to replace or change all surfaces in the room to give

it a new look. A simple paint job and a new marble island countertop can transform a modest kitchen with very little effort. Or perhaps your laminate countertops are showing their age; they may be the only surface you need to update to keep the kitchen looking neat and trim.

Regardless, the possibilities are mind-boggling. Take the kitchen floor, for example. Fifty years ago, the choices were pretty much limited to linoleum or ceramic tile. Now you can choose from a

▼ **MIX AND MATCH TO FOOL THE EYE.** A painted backsplash? Custom inlay? Nope. The backsplash is a laminate surface, as is the counter, but with brushed gold aluminum strips inlaid for a unique look. Although these products can all be found at retail, this type of use is a signature look that could have easily come right out of a professional designer's workbook. There simply is no excuse to settle for ho-hum surfaces in your kitchen.

STYLIZE SEDATE WITH A SOLID-COLOR SURFACE. One of the key decisions in choosing a countertop will be whether to choose patterns or a solid color. Although there are many intriguing patterned countertop materials, a solid color offers a clean, sleek, refined, and low-key appearance that is ideal for a contemporary kitchen such as this one. The gray quartz countertop here is super-durable, and a beveled edge profile like the one on this counter gives it a nice understated detail.

bevy of durable, beautiful, and easy-to-install options. They include vinyl sheet and tile products, laminates that look like stone or wood surfaces, wood flooring, and stone tiles in just about any size or shape.

Countertop choices are no less expansive. These days, you can have a lovely old-fashioned ceramic tile counter if that's where your tastes lie. But you can also opt for a more contemporary quartz surface in a look that mimics marble, granite, or other high-end stone. Or perhaps you're searching for the kind of luxury those real stone surfaces offer. They're widely available if you're willing to spend the money. If your budget is a little more modest, and the idea of a "green" countertop appeals to you, take a look at the stunning and surprising recycled paper or glass options on the marketplace. Whatever your design taste, budget, and needs, you're certain to find more than one countertop option that will do the job beautifully.

Sift through the images on these pages to get a sense of the options. Among the many examples of different surfaces shown here, you're certain to hone in on winners that make the most sense for your kitchen, your pocketbook, and your design preferences.

GO DEEP FOR DRAMA. A thick countertop makes for an impressive appearance, as evidenced by this quartz surface. Quartz countertops can be manufactured in a variety of thicknesses and can include custom elements like the special long, skinny sink in this island. The look is slick and contemporary. However, thicker countertops are usually limited to islands, because base cabinet heights around the perimeter of the room restrict countertop thickness.

▶ **BLEND DIFFERENT COLORS OF THE SAME MATERIAL FOR AN INTRIGUING MIX.** These solid surface countertops look like the vanilla and chocolate versions, because the mottling and patterns are so similar. That helps them look natural together, but it's also wise when mixing counters in this way to use the same material, as has been done here. If the counters are too dissimilar, the look may be overly jarring—a problem that is extremely hard to fix after installation.

USE QUARTZ TO DRESS UP A MODERN KITCHEN. White is the typical color for a modern kitchen, but you can add a bit of visual interest to an otherwise stark white room with an elegantly patterned quartz countertop. The wraparound island countertop shown here is all about sharp edges, a sleek surface, and sophisticated "barely there" mottling. It teases the eye and provides a bit of relief from the other bright white surfaces. It's also a tough surface that can withstand all kinds of food prep and any other abuse you can throw at it.

ACCOMMODATE MULTIPLE OPENINGS IN A SINGLE SURFACE WITH QUARTZ. Because a quartz countertop can be fabricated to just about any specifications, you can design a countertop to contain double sinks, a cooktop, and more. This long surface keeps all the fixtures in order and looks sharp doing it. It also provides a surface that will hold up well to high traffic and lots of use and will be easy to clean at the end of the day—an extremely important feature if you're opting for an all-white counter!

▲ **UNIFY THE KITCHEN DESIGN WITH COUNTERTOPS.** Different areas of this kitchen—oversized island, alcove oven area, and the sink—are visually tied together with the use of a stylish quartz countertop material. Although it looks like marble, this material is fabricated to suit the space—no mining necessary. It's also a great choice for multiple areas where different tasks will be performed; from the waterlogged area around the sink to the food prep done on the island, the material will hold up.

▲ **GO VERTICAL IN STYLE WITH QUARTZ.** As much as it makes for a great countertop, a quartz slab can also serve as an easy-to-clean backsplash. The cooktop area shown here is kept neat and trim with a flat induction unit centered in a quartz countertop, with matching backsplash. It's a sleek look that can be executed easily wherever a quartz countertop butts up against a wall. It's also pretty simple to install.

◄ **GO MONOCHROME BY MATCHING SINK TO COUNTER.** Here, a black laminate countertop is perfectly complemented with a glossy black sink and chic gooseneck faucet with valve handle and sprayer sharing a single deckplate. The faucet provides the sparkle, while the sink and counter create a dramatic black statement. Today's sinks come in a wide range of colors and finishes, so you should have no trouble matching yours to the countertop you want.

▲ **ADD PATTERN TO A CLEAN WHITE LOOK WITH QUARTZ.** Quartz surfaces have a lot going for them—they are durable, require little in the way of maintenance, and are solid surfaces so that they can be used with undermount sinks. The countertops are cut and modified in much the same way stone surfaces are, but at a lower cost. And, best of all, they come in an incredible range of appearances, including the marble-mimicking look here, which suits the otherwise simple white background.

BUY STONE WITHOUT PAYING FOR STONE. Modern laminate counters offer incredible representations of other materials. The faux granite surface here is not just a repeating pattern as was used in the past. The manufacturer has gone to great pains to re-create the unique graining variations in an actual slab of granite. The result is a look that would be hard to discern from actual granite unless you were the homeowner or installer. Choose a laminate like this—and order an ogee edge profile like the one shown here—and you'll have all the beauty of a real granite surface at a fraction of the cost.

◀ **MIX AND MATCH COUNTERTOP MATERIALS WHERE THE LOOKS NATURALLY BLEND.** This black counter may look like granite, but it's quartz. The beautiful reflective surface grabs attention, but really pops against a white lower counter that is laminate. The teak cabinet drawer fronts are also laminate, and all three surfaces are offered by the same manufacturer. That makes them not only beautiful together, but easy to buy as a package.

▶ **FIND THE UNUSUAL—AND SPECTACULAR— AMONG MODERN LAMINATES.** Today's laminate countertops come in an astounding diversity of patterns and colors that gives you the means to affect just about any look you might want in your kitchen for a very reasonable cost. This laminate countertop is on the wild side of the spectrum, featuring the stunning appearance of petrified wood in a thick profile that makes the counter look like one gigantic slab of old-growth forest. It's unique, well suited to the cabinets and space, and tremendously eye-catching.

▷ **SPEND LESS FOR QUARRY STONE.** Few looks say luxury like the appearance of a marble surface in a well-appointed kitchen. You'd be hard-pressed to find anyone who didn't recognize these counters as marble, and the look is undeniably posh. But it's also undeniably affordable. The surfaces are all extremely convincing reproductions of marble surfaces. It's a surefire look that really makes the kitchen shine. Reproducing the appearance of high-end quarry stone is one of the things modern laminates do best—and it's a great way to have the look and impression of marble with a much lower cost.

▽ **LET LAMINATE REPRODUCTIONS TAKE YOU WHERE THE ACTUAL MATERIALS CAN'T GO.** A 12-foot-long butcher-block counter would be an incredibly difficult surface to fabricate even if you were willing and able to foot the bill or craft it yourself. But make that countertop out of a faux butcher-block laminate and you've achieved the look you wanted with less expense and hassle. This beautiful countertop is almost indistinguishable from the real thing, and fits right into the look of this industrial loft kitchen.

PICK CRISP, CLEAN, AND SEDATE COUNTER DESIGNS WHERE THEY'RE MEANT TO SUPPORT OTHER PLAYERS IN THE KITCHEN. The sophisticated gray solid-surface counters in this kitchen not only match the floating shelves, but they allow the classic subway tile to pop and serve as stages for the stunning, state-of-the-art bar and kitchen sink faucets. Sometimes, it's as important to use solid supporting players as it is to integrate a design star.

▶ HIDE THE SEAM. Modern laminate manufacturers have developed a lot of ways to conceal edge seams—the primary giveaway that the counter is actually a laminate and not a stone surface. The illusion is kept complete with this countertop through the use of a bullnose front edge. This is only one of many edge profiles laminate countertop suppliers can create, but all are designed to minimize any seams so that the counter seems to be something it is not.

▶ **GET GRANITE FOR GORGEOUS LOOKS.** Granite is the most popular quarry stone used for countertops in the home and for good reason. It comes in a range of colors and surface patterns, each more elegant than the last. With minimal maintenance, the countertop will last just about forever and it can endure heat, knife blades, and all manner of abuse without looking timeworn. These particular countertops are actually granite shells, made of pieces leftover from the fabrication of solid granite surfaces. Although they are less expensive than a solid surface, they are every bit as durable and beautiful—and available in every color and pattern granite offers.

▲ **ENLARGE WITH GRANITE.** Granite, like other luxury surface materials, is perfect for small spaces, bringing a touch of luxury for far less than it would cost to outfit a larger kitchen. The black granite used here provides a dramatic counterpoint to the largely white room—a color choice that was meant to keep the small kitchen visually large. The elegance of the countertops is well matched to the glass-front cabinets and high-end light fixture.

▲ **BRING A BACKSPLASH TO LIFE WITH PATTERNED TILE IN COMPLEMENTARY COLORS.** The wall surface here has been covered in textured-glass tile in the neutrals that match the cabinets. Notice that a geometric shape has been used for the drawer pulls, purposely contrasting the flowing lines of the backsplash. The pulls and handles are ultra-elegant finishing touches on the cabinets and create a calm visual below the busy backsplash.

MAKE IT SPECIAL WITH MARBLE. Although this craftsman-style country kitchen has a lovely understated appeal with its cream-yellow color and true-to-form cabinetry, the marble countertops put the design over the top. The white-and-green veined marble is perfect for the space, and because the kitchen is fairly modest in size, splurging on marble countertop surfaces didn't break the bank for the homeowner. This kitchen proves that the right marble surfaces in the right place provides a lot more design bang for whatever bucks you might have spent.

▶ **MATCH A TABLE FOR A COORDINATED LOOK.** The stunning, stainless steel-topped dining table in this kitchen sets the tone for the countertops. Stainless steel was an insightful choice because it carries through the theme of a high-end, serious cooking area anchored by the restaurant-quality range. The countertops are easy to clean and a sleek accent to the frameless European-style cabinets and designer pendant lighting.

▲ **BRIGHTEN SMALL SPACES WITH STAINLESS STEEL SURFACES.** This tiny kitchen is kept visually open with the use of light-colored frameless cabinetry and stainless steel counters, backsplashes, and appliances. The metal surfaces reflect a maximum of light and provide a clean, uncluttered appearance. They are also easy to clean, which can be a crucial factor in small busy kitchens.

▲ **LET STAINLESS STEEL DOMINATE.** Clad a large island like this entirely in stainless steel and the result is a clean, inviting kitchen design. Complement the stainless steel with white walls and ceilings, and incorporate a complementary flooring such as this stunning, light-colored surface. This floor looks like wood, but it's not. It's actually incredibly detailed glazed porcelain tile—a feature that adds immeasurably to the chic look of this kitchen.

▲ **CONFUSE THE EYE WITH ZINC.** This may look like stainless steel, but it is actually polished zinc. Zinc has been used for the countertops in European bars for over a century, but it also makes a great kitchen countertop material. The installer can seal the surface of the zinc to protect it, but you might be wiser to let the natural zinc surface be. It can be affected by skin oils, lemon juice, and other materials, giving the surface a patina and marks that many people feel are its most alluring traits. It's on par with the cost of a stainless steel surface, but much more distinctive.

◄ **SURPRISE WITH WOOD.** Thin, whitewashed wood paneling makes for a stunning backsplash in this kitchen. The surface provides a wonderful backdrop that contrasts the more low-key solid surface countertop, and elegant brushed steel faucet with pull-down head and single lever handle. The contrasts create constant visual interest in the space.

INTRODUCE BOLD ACCENTS WITH GLASS COUNTERTOPS. Because these countertops are produced using glass from a variety of sources, they come in almost every color of the rainbow, including vivid hues like the blue of this surface. You don't need to commit to the color throughout the space; you can incorporate the material as a small section of countertop like a work surface next to the cooktop, as shown here. One of the advantages of this type of countertop is that it can be fabricated to nearly any shape, such as the partial dogleg at the back edge of this counter.

COMPLEMENT OTHER COUNTERTOPS WITH RECYCLED GLASS. The busy patterns of a recycled-glass surface can overwhelm a kitchen with several large expanses of countertop. But use the material in one area of the kitchen—like the breakfast bar L in this room—and you create a dynamic accent that adds life to an otherwise subtle kitchen design. Notice that the designer selected a recycled-glass surface in muted grays, a choice that dials back the visual power of the material and blends it more seamlessly with the other solid-color countertops.

OPT FOR RECYCLED GLASS COUNTERS FOR MAXIMUM PATTERN AND COLOR. Although dynamic color is the most obvious selling point for recycled-glass countertops, these surfaces also provide the opportunity to introduce mesmerizing patterns into the kitchen. Choose the color carefully as this homeowner did, so that the hues blend naturally with other tones in the room—the dominant brown in this countertop complements the cabinet below. Get the color right, and the pattern becomes a riveting design element. This countertop illustrates the intense interest that can be created by large and small pieces of glass randomly intermingled.

▲ **EXPLORE NEW TECHNOLOGY FOR STUNNING COUNTERTOPS.**
This cutting-edge fused-glass surface is created with a combination of new and recycled glasses, creating an unusual and exciting appearance. Manufacturers continue to explore new horizons with existing materials to create spectacular countertop surfaces like this. Expand your search if what you're after is a design focal point surface for your kitchen.

▲ **MATCH GLASS WITH GLASS.** A recycled-glass countertop is a natural choice to pair with other glass design elements in the kitchen. The surface here was selected in a color that blends with the colors of the glass tile backsplash, the green glass inserts in the upper cabinets, and the appliance front panel. The wealth of reflective surfaces make this small space seem bright and airy, and the countertop and backsplash ensure that it is also easy to keep clean.

▷ **HAVE FUN WITH RECYCLED GLASS.** Because they can be blended with just about any mix of colors, you can create a jubilant, smile-making kitchen design around the right recycled glass surface. This L-shaped counter combines a mix of carnival colors that are moderated by the white substrate. It's an incredibly fun look, but not so busy that it's overwhelming. If your kitchen design is a little eclectic and you're willing to take the plunge into whimsy, this could be the perfect countertop choice.

CLEANING KITCHEN SURFACES

Today's kitchens often incorporate two or more completely different surfaces to create visual interest and embellish the room's design. A tile backsplash may back a solid-surface countertop. Or quartz counters might be paired with a marble island top. Keeping those varied surfaces looking their best is a matter of using the right cleaning materials in the right way. Be careful how you treat and clean your kitchen surfaces and they will likely last the life of the kitchen.

• MARBLE. Marble counters are a rarity in the kitchen because of their expense. If you're fortunate enough to own marble counters, wall tiles, or flooring, take steps to avoid stains that could mar the exceptionally luxurious appearance. Any acidic substance, from lemon juice to balsamic vinegar, is the enemy. Clean them off the surface immediately. For general cleaning, you can use one of the many cleaning products labeled specifically for marble, or make your own with a little dish soap in warm water. Wipe the mixture across the surface and then follow with a clean moist cloth, removing all soap residue. Buff with a clean dry towel.

Marble is susceptible to staining, and removing stains can be part of keeping the counters looking their best. The solution depends on the stain and usually involves creating a slightly abrasive poultice. However, for best results contact a local quarry stone vendor about the specific stain. You should also regularly reseal marble surfaces. Resealants are widely available at large home centers. Follow the manufacturer's directions.

• GRANITE. This handsome stone surface is less porous than marble, but you should still clean up spills as soon as they happen. Use specialized granite cleaners if you prefer (specific products are often recommended and even sold by the countertop installer), but you'll most likely realize just as reliable results using a mild mixture of warm water and dish soap. In any case, avoid acidic or caustic cleaners,

and don't expose the surface to acidic foodstuffs such as vinegar and lemon juice. Granite counters should be resealed every two to four years by a professional.

• LAMINATE. Prevention is key if you want to keep a laminate countertop not only clean, but looking its best. It's essential to wipe up spills quickly because laminate surfaces stain easily. Although you can clean the counter with a mixture of warm water and dish soap, you may want use a store-bought counter cleaner because flooding seams around sinks or edges can cause swelling and separation between the laminate surface and the underlying bonding structure.

• QUARTZ. Quartz countertops are durable and easy to clean, requiring little more than warm water and a clean cloth or paper towel. If something stronger is needed, use a non-bleach cleaner labeled for use on quartz surfaces. Always be diligent about cleaning up spills and splashes before they dry, to avoid stains.

• CONCRETE. Don't be fooled by the impressive look of a polished concrete counter; the surface requires attention and careful cleaning. Don't use abrasive pads or cleaners on the surface, and avoid acidic substances. Some installers even recommend monthly waxing. However, another school of thought holds that the imperfections that crop up over time and use only increase the intriguing visual appeal of concrete surfaces. Decide for yourself.

◀ **USE COUNTER SURFACES TO CREATE CONTINUITY THROUGH MULTIPLE AREAS IN THE KITCHEN.** This eclectic kitchen design includes the same countertop material used in two counters, an island, and the kitchen table. Although it looks like marble, marble would have been prohibitively expensive to use for so many surfaces. Instead, these are quartz surfaces—every bit as beautiful, durable, and even lower-maintenance. But the principle translates; this design technique would work with wood, ceramic tile, laminate, or any kind of stone.

▲ **COLOR YOUR KITCHEN "SOPHISTICATED" WITH VOLCANIC ROCK.** These countertops come in 16 glossy and 16 matte colors, ranging from magnificent reds to the chic elegance of the blue shown here. The colors are fired onto the volcanic rock surface, creating an alluring visual depth that is unique among countertop materials. Although the bolder colors are usually used sparingly, the more understated shades like this can transform a kitchen and serve as countertops throughout even a large room.

▲ **INCORPORATE NIFTY BUILT-IN EXTRAS WITH VOLCANIC ROCK COUNTERS.** The fabrication process used to create these countertops allows for special features to be crafted right into the structure of the countertop. This bright white sink counter is evidence of what can be done with the material; a stepped-down sink section was made with integrated drainboards on either side of the sink. The finished edge allowed for an undermount sink, and custom holes accommodate a high-end faucet with independent handles.

▶ **OUTFIT HIGH-USE AREAS WITH DURABLE VOLCANIC ROCK.** This countertop material really comes into its own in prep and cooking areas. The enamel glaze that colors the surface is fired onto the rock at temperatures around 1,000°F, so it's nearly indestructible. It will hold up to knives, hot pots, and even bleach cleansers without a mar or a stain. A high-use location, such as the island prep surface next to a cooktop in this kitchen, is the perfect opportunity to let this material shine.

▶ **DON'T FEAR A BUSY LOOK.** Backsplashes are such tightly defined wall spaces that you can easily use a busy pattern, like the Moroccan-inspired ceramic tile shown here, in the area. A beautiful, patterned quartz countertop is a calmer counterpoint to the backsplash tiles, and the rest of the kitchen has been done in solid colors to create a pleasant, moderating backdrop.

▽ **COUNTER THE BACKSPLASH.** Although the stunning backsplash in this chic modern kitchen may look like coordinated tile, it's actually a quartz surface just like the counters. Quartz is ideal for backsplash areas for the same reasons the material makes such a great countertop: cleanability, durability, and amazingly diverse surface appearances. Keep in mind that you can use quartz backsplashes with other types of counters—just match the appearances.

GO BEYOND BUTCHER-BLOCK FOR INCREDIBLE STYLE. Wood plank counters are a step up from the common and folksy butcher-block. Not only do hardwoods offer fascinating intricate grain patterns, they are also prime candidates for custom cutting and fabrication into ornate shapes like the island countertop in this kitchen. The outline of the counter echoes the shape of the base legs, and presents an incredible edge profile that helps boost the stately cred of the entire kitchen design. A dark brown finish was an inspired choice and, although the wood should not be used as a cutting surface, it is resistant to other abuse and moisture.

▲ **ADD SHARP, CLEAN LINES WITH RECYCLED-PAPER SURFACES.**
Although the edges of this type of countertop can be
fabricated with many different profiles (a carbide tip router
is all it takes), the countertops come from the manufacturer
with a sleek flat front. Use the plain edge in a kitchen like
this one, with crisp lines defining the design, and bright
white halogen lights highlighting the details in the surfaces.
Keeping the original edge profile also makes installing the
countertop a much easier project.

▶ **GO ECO-FRIENDLY AND HEALTHY.** This satiny surface may
look like slate, but it's actually a recycled-paper countertop.
Made from 100 percent post-consumer waste combined
with natural binders and pigments, the surface is remarkably
durable. It won't stain, it is not susceptible to moisture
damage, and cuts or abrasions can be sanded out. It will also
hold up to a lot of wear and tear. You'll find recycled paper
countertops in a range of neutrals and earth tones, at prices
competitive with other options. And the counters don't have
a negative impact on indoor air quality, so you'll be doing
your family—and the environment—a favor.

◁ **SHAPE TO SUIT.** Because they are colored uniformly all the way through, recycled-paper countertops can be cut to many different shapes. This curving tiered countertop is an example of what can be done with the material. The top counter surface is also a thicker-than-normal panel—the material is sold in different thickness. Choose based on the look you want. These properties make recycled-paper countertops adaptable to a wide range of kitchen styles and personal design preferences.

▲ **GET EDGY WITH RECYCLED-PAPER SURFACES.** Some recycled-paper countertops are offered with special exposed edge treatments, like the sample shown here. Compressed layers are shown in cutaway edges, and add a delicate bit of visual interest to the side of the countertop. This edge treatment is available in different colors, all of which complement the top color, making it easy to coordinate the look in your kitchen. Details like these are a way to put your own signature on the kitchen design.

▲ **PICK A FINISH THAT SUITS YOU.** One of the wonderful things about a recycled-paper countertop is that you can use the satin finish with which the material is manufactured, or use finishing products—available from the manufacturer—to create a high-gloss surface. Use it where you want to brighten the naturally toned-down color, or where you want to amplify the available light in the room. Note that these counters are also great for use with undermount sinks like the one shown here. Seal the edges and there will be no problems with moisture infiltration.

◄ **PLAY WITH SHEENS TO MAKE A COUNTERTOP POP.** This glossy quartz surface is a wonderful stage for an elegant chrome gooseneck faucet. But it really comes into its own when contrasted with a matte backsplash of mosaic tile, and a cabinet run of Shaker lower cabinets in matte, monocolor paint. Simple contrasts like this can add tons of visual excitement and bring a whole kitchen to life.

► **SEPARATE YOUR ISLAND WITH A HANDY BUTCHER-BLOCK TOP.** Islands are some of the most common locations for butcher-block countertops because they are usually centers of activities such as food prep as well as being visual centers of the room. A butcher-block island counter makes the fixture eminently usable and warms up the room. This makes it a great surface for a room with stainless steel counters or any other countertop materials that are reflective and visually "cold."

▲ **FORM AN ISLAND OF QUARTZ.** A wraparound structure such as this is a common use for quartz surfaces because they have precise crisp lines and the material is relatively easy to work with (this type of surface would be incredibly difficult to craft out of marble or granite). Although these types of islands are left open underneath, essentially forming an upside-down U, adding a divider knee wall as with this island gives the entire piece more visual weight and helps support the long run of unbroken countertop.

◄ **SAY "SERIOUS" WITH A STEEL BACKSPLASH.** Stainless steel can serve as a startlingly unusual backsplash, one that sends the message that the kitchen is meant for cooking. A sumptuous quartz countertop adds to the impression, adding beautiful pattern under the crisp silver surface of the backsplash. Both countertop and backsplash are smart choices where cleanup is concerned, and both are extremely durable, so splashes and spills won't leave stains. The backsplash also ties the entire kitchen together, providing a visual link between the range and other appliances and the walls of the kitchen.

MAKE A SOPHISTICATED STATEMENT WITH A BACKSPLASH WALL. The green glass tiles behind this high-end electric induction range are manufactured with a color backing that gives the glass surface a uniform color. Using oversized tiles helps tie the wall design to the rest of the room, because the grid of lines mimics the clean, linear aspect of the cabinets in the space, as well as the shape of the other design elements such as the range hood. It's a super sleek, eye-catching appearance that was simple and easy to create.

▲ **VISUALLY SEPARATE THE BACKSPLASH WALL.** Consider any backsplash area—even if it's an entire wall—as a canvas of specific dimensions. You add visual depth and definition to the kitchen as a whole by separating that wall surface from others. Here, the surface finish, texture, color, and overall appearance of a wall of glass tiles is not only an incredible attention-grabber, it also sets the wall apart. Although many different types of bond pattern could have been used with this tile, straight lines serve the kitchen's design best.

◄ **WARM UP WITH WOOD.** A wood backsplash is an unexpected treat for the eye, and wood in a dark stain like the cabinet fronts and backsplash in this kitchen provide a foil for features like the light, solid-color counter; white accents and appliances; and stunning, well-outfitted storage cabinets that replace more traditional models. The look is clean without being sterile.

▶ **TIE A ROOM TOGETHER BY EXTENDING A BACKSPLASH TREATMENT.** You can unify a kitchen design by covering entire walls with the same surface material you use for the backsplash. The black mosaic tile in this room would make a stunning backsplash, but used across two walls, it makes the red cabinetry pop and provides the perfect backdrop to luxury stainless steel appliances. It's also a lovely complement to the smaller mosaic tile used on the floor. This is a very effective design technique, especially in smaller kitchens.

◀ **CREATE A BACKSPLASH ACCENT WALL.** By using the entire wall as a backsplash, you increase the visual power of the feature—well worth considering when you're covering the surface with hip glass tiles like those shown here. The tiles used in this kitchen include a range of shapes and neutral hues, all of which complement the brown walls, cabinets, and countertops. It's a perfectly coordinated look, but one that puts the focus on the accent wall, proving that you can never go too big with a backsplash surface.

◄ **TEXTURE YOUR BACKSPLASH TO INVITE TOUCH AND COMPLIMENTS.** A little added texture only heightens the look of a high-style backsplash like this. By interspersing textured tiles in shades of the same color, the homeowner creates endless fascination for the eye and a treat for the fingers (as long as the burners aren't lit). The trick is to either use all textured tiles, or use a mixture with colors that blend seamlessly. That way you'll impress your guests without overwhelming the eye.

▲ **MAKE MOSAIC MAGIC.** Don't settle for plain, ordinary mosaics on your backsplash. Look a little further and you'll find very special mosaic tiles (sometimes special order) that will create a simple stunning vertical surface. These tiles have a gold-leafed surface that shimmers in luxuriant tones and changes appearance under different lights. All its different tones blend perfectly with the elegant laminate countertop and brown cabinets. You can also choose from metal mosaics and upscale quarry stone versions.

◄ **REFINE THE LOOK WITH MONOCHROMATIC TILE.** You can do a lot with a few simple shades of a neutral color, especially when you use tiles in different shapes, like the glass tiles covering this backsplash and wall. Some manufacturers make this easier than it looks, by joining the tiles on standardized sheets that are easy to install. But in any case, the subtle shadings supply just enough visual interest to add to the kitchen design without creating visual noise.

▲ **MATCH UNUSUAL FLOORING TO AN UNUSUAL DESIGN.** This spectacular kitchen features a quote relief along the wall-top molding, a map of London as a backsplash, and period-style lamps and drapes, all topped off with luxury, pro-quality stainless steel appliances. It's an eclectic but thoughtful design that is perfectly set off by a hexagonal mosaic tile floor. The floor's character seems right in keeping with all the other face-forward, distinctive design elements, and the white coloring ensures that the space is not overwhelmed with dark tones.

▶ **BE TIMELESS WITH STONE TILE.** Flooring like the soapstone tiles in this kitchen will not only last the life of the kitchen, the look never goes out of style. Although you can opt for granite, marble, or ceramics if you're after pronounced color or patterns, soapstone is a great choice for an understated floor underfoot, one that features very subtle variations and a forgiving surface that is low maintenance. The look of sandstone also transcends design styles; this floor would be just as at home in a contemporary setting as it is in this Euro-country kitchen.

◀ **OPEN UP A KITCHEN WITH BLONDE WOOD.** There is a singular beauty to a blonde wood floor like the Normandy oak that graces this sleek and fun kitchen. The floor matches the open and airy feeling of the rest of the kitchen with its glass doors and copious window exposure and high cathedral ceilings. A floor such as this can be dressed up with bold rugs, but left alone it's like a constant breath of fresh air in the space.

▼ **PLAY WITH PLANKS TO CONTRAST AN OTHERWISE CLEAN, SPARE KITCHEN.** Wood plank flooring, especially any featuring wide planks like the one shown here, increases visual interest in the room and offers an incredible variety in the surface appearance. This floor presents different shadings, graining, and finishes, all of which contrasts the uniform lines and solid colors that define the rest of the kitchen.

STICK WITH SHEET VINYL. Modern versions of this durable sheet flooring continue to be immensely popular because in addition to being affordable and easy to install, the material now comes in amazingly realistic surface appearances from finely grained wood planks to the travertine stone surface here. The floor is so detailed that the grout lines look aged. And, unlike real stone, the floor will be warm underfoot in the winter months.

CREATE A STUNNING STAGE. A porcelain floor with the appearance of white wood doesn't call attention to itself right off the bat. But look at it for any length of time, and the fine detail of this tiled surface makes a strong impression. This home is situated in a warm region, making porcelain a great choice for an underfoot surface; the material keeps cool in the heat and is incredibly durable. It's also easy to clean and ages well.

▶ **CONTRAST FOR DRAMA. GOING HARDWOOD?** Consider darker tones from walnut through ebony. Although the wood grain and warmth underfoot are key selling points, a dark wood floor can provide a fascinating visual contrast to the usually white or light hues used in a kitchen. Keep in mind that if you find the darker shade doesn't work, you can always refinish the floor and still enjoy the benefits of a wood surface.

◀ **PICK A PATTERN TO EXCITE THE EYE.** A simple, white country kitchen is lovely in its own right, but add a detailed floor design and you ramp up the visual impact in the space. This floor is vinyl sheet, a material that comes in a range of dynamic patterns—and even textures. Although the pattern itself is busy, notice that only two colors are used, and the tones remain neutral. That means the floor will work with most colors that the homeowner might want to introduce into the room.

⊙⊙⊙⊙⊙●⊙⊙⊙⊙⊙⊙⊙⊙

▶ **SYNC SUBTLE WITH SIMPLE TILES.** The very basic cream-colored ceramic tile in this kitchen is perfect for the low-key, neutral-colored design. It complements the light-hued frameless base cabinets and the off-white upper cabinets. It also creates the ideal stage to show off an upscale stainless steel gas range. Using neutral colors and minimal patterns and lines is a great way to showcase high-end appliances or special features in the kitchen.

▼ **REINFORCE RUSTIC STYLE WITH TRAVERTINE TILES.** This particular stone tile is closely associated with Italian Tuscan style, as well as other continental country styles. It's both a sophisticated and old-world rural look that adds flavor to a country kitchen. Embellish a kitchen design like this with backsplash tiles that match the natural earth tones in the floor, such as the rectangular porcelain tiles used on the wall behind this sink. Add a few dozen bottles of wine for a particularly authentic look and dining pleasure.

◀ **MAKE YOUR KITCHEN HEALTHY WITH MARMOLEUM®.** Marmoleum is the modern version of linoleum and comes in easy-to-install tiles called "click" flooring. The number of colors, patterns and looks available in marmoleum are incredible, and a simple color blend such as the yellow-and-white scheme in this country kitchen is just one of many possible combinations. Marmoleum, like linoleum, is antibacterial, doesn't off-gas any volatile compounds, and is made of natural ingredients, all of which makes it one of the greenest flooring materials you can choose.

▲ **TAKE YOUR KITCHEN DESIGN IN A NEW DIRECTION.** Vinyl tiles like these are easy to install and give you a chance to put your own imprint on your kitchen design. By mixing and matching tiles with the same coloration—and by mixing the direction of the "grain" in the tiles—you have endless options for making the look of your kitchen floor totally unique. No matter how it looks, you'll be saving money with a custom appearance.

▲ ▶ **COMBINE COMFORT WITH LUXURY.** This modern space is perfectly outfitted with a beautiful slate floor . . . except that the floor is vinyl. Notice that even the texture is correct— it's almost impossible to tell it from actual stone. Well, until you walk across the floor and feel the cushion and warmth underfoot. Dropped glassware and dishes are also less likely to break on this version than they would on a true slate floor.

▶ **NEUTRALIZE FLOOR COLORS TO MAKE THEM AS ADAPTABLE AS POSSIBLE.** This floor is vinyl tile, which is available in all kinds of surface appearances. The stone graining shown here is a nice look, and the mid-tone browns will work with the kitchen even if paint schemes, color accents, and furnishings change over time. A neutral color is always a safe bet for a kitchen floor.

▲ **RUN PLANKS IN A DIRECTION THAT MAKES SENSE FOR THE KITCHEN DESIGN.** This wood plank floor is actually laminate, but the homeowner still had to decide which direction to run the planks. By pointing them toward the sink and range, the eye is naturally drawn to the center of action in the space. You can lead the viewer through any kitchen design using a subtle device like flooring direction.

◄ **ENJOY THE WARMTH OF WOOD WITHOUT THE WORK.** Wood kitchen floors are gorgeous and perfectly in keeping with the country kitchen style of this room. But save yourself the effort and expense by buying a vinyl version like the one shown here. It looks exactly like a wood floor, but is completely waterproof and far less expensive. What's more, it will never need to be sanded and refinished.

▶ **BE ENVIRONMENTALLY FRIENDLY WITH YOUR FLOOR.** Cork is an entirely natural substance that is moisture resistant and easy to clean. Cork tiles like these are usually given a natural finish to allow the character of the material to really shine. There are many nontoxic sealants and finishing products for cork floors, which will help the floor last a good long time and look good for its entire life. All that, and a warm, super cushy surface underfoot account for the growing popularity of this intriguing flooring material.

▼ **CREATE VISUAL CONTINUITY BETWEEN ROOMS BY RUNNING A COMMON FLOOR OVER THE KITCHEN AND LIVING AREAS.** This distinctive wide-plank herringbone floor is an attention-getter in any room, but it's especially effective at tying the kitchen with the living room in a successful open floor plan. This type of application makes both rooms seem open and airy, a perception that is reinforced by the abundant light and bright white that dominates the kitchen.

DRAMATIZE YOUR KITCHEN. When carefully stained, cork tiles can take on the alluring appearance of timeworn stone. The floor here is a clear example of the deep, rich coloring that can be achieved by staining and finishing a cork floor with an aged appearance in mind. Cork floors are also a doable DIY project, even when you want to include a special feature like the border in this floor. All it takes is a little planning and bit of work, and you could have floor that mimics stone but feels like walking on a cloud.

▲ **LEVERAGE THE TIMELESS QUALITY OF A
CLASSIC STRIP FLOOR.** This light oak floor will
never go out of style. Installed and finished
correctly, it will be durable, even in the
presence of moisture and spills. When it finally
shows its age, it's a simple project to refinish
the floor and you can even re-stain it for a
different look. Properly maintained, you can
amortize over the life of the floor to realize a
real value and a long-lasting beauty.

▶ **GET YOUR COUNTRY STYLE ON WITH WOOD
FLOORING.** A themed kitchen like this, with
authentic recessed panel cabinets and antiqued
pulls, latches, and hinges, calls for true wood
floor. The dusty yellow of the cabinets is
complemented perfectly by the light tones of
the oak strip flooring. The floor seems almost
like an extension of the wood-finished island,
and it provides a visual stage for the beautifully
colored cabinets.

LET WOOD SET A WARM TONE. This kitchen features a sharp, clean look with stunning white-trim cabinets and quartz countertops. Gloss white paint and a shiny countertop surface can lead the design to be somewhat cold, but the use of a handsome wood floor—along with a handy extendable wood cutting board—lends warmth and visual depth to the room and provides a comfortable surface underfoot. The surface slightly cushions impacts and can save the occasional dropped glass or plate.

STAY ON TREND WITH A GRAY HARDWOOD FLOOR. Gray is the new ebony in wood floors, and a deep, rich gray like this one will hide dirt and scuffs, and will age well. You're not likely to tire of the floor, and it will go as well with any new color scheme as it does with the beige that dominates this kitchen. The darkness of the stain helps all the lighter elements in the kitchen pop and look sharper and more vibrant.

▶ **EXPLOIT WOOD STAINS FOR UNIQUE LOOKS.** Wood floors certainly look handsome finished natural, but staining a wood surface an unusual shade is a great way to get even more design bang out of the flooring. The gray stain used on this kitchen floor provides the perfect stage for an upscale, reserved contemporary kitchen design, and the choice of satin—rather than gloss—stain is inspired. The floor contrasts the lighter cabinets and furniture in the space, creating a wonderful visual balance with just enough dynamic tension to keep things interesting.

◀ **DRESS UP A FLOOR WITH BORDERS AND INSETS.** Although these features take a little planning to install correctly, a medallion, border, or other inset area, like the base border around the island in this kitchen, can be a real show-stopper. Whenever you use a border or other inlaid design, the point is to make it as pronounced as possible. That's why the homeowner decided on different woods and different finishes for the inlaid design in this floor. If you're going to the trouble and expense of installing a special flooring feature, flaunt it!

SAVE MONEY WITH LAMINATES. Have your eye set on a nice oak-strip floor, like this one? Well, you need to adjust your eyes and prepare for thrift, because this is laminate flooring. Created with a photographic layer underneath a durable clear layer of plastic, laminates come in a range of surface appearances, but the most popular are wood. The look is convincing and installing the floor is a fairly easy weekend project for the moderately accomplished DIYer.

SELECT A LAMINATE FOR THE LONG HAUL. The incredible variety of surface appearances means you have lots of choices to select from when shopping for laminates. But in a basic contemporary kitchen like this, it's wise to choose a look—like the mid-range oak-strip-style laminate here—that will continue to work in your kitchen design as you change or update it. A floor like this is durable enough to last a decade and will work with cabinets, countertops, and walls from light to dark, traditional to modern.

STYLISH KITCHEN STORAGE

Classy Cabinets

Specialty Cabinet Storage

Handsome Racks & Shelves

Storage is an ever-present necessity in the kitchen. So many food-stuffs and different cooking equipment have to find a home in the kitchen that it's rare you have all the storage space you need. But incorporating storage can be frustrating process of maximizing available space to store changing quantities and types of containers and small items. Oh, and it's all got to look good too.

Thank goodness that manufacturers have lots of experience combining style and function—starting with ubiquitous cabinetry. Kitchen cabinets are offered in every design style, size, finish, and configuration imaginable.

But the truth is, you may not be looking to completely replace your existing cabinetry. That doesn't mean you can't update your kitchen storage. Shelves are easy additions to any kitchen and can be incredibly handy places for good-looking items such as glassware or gourmet food containers. You can also retrofit the inside of cabinets or add specialty cabinets for specific storage.

The possibilities don't end with your cabinets. You can turn to a host of options for storing different cookware and essentials. These include pot racks, spice racks, wine racks, and more.

Whether you're entirely redesigning the space, or just trying to freshen up the kitchen's look, begin with what you need to store. Getting things out in the open, hanging from hooks or racks is a good strategy if it suits your particular design style. Adding shelves or moveable baskets or boxes is a great way to incorporate additional storage that can accommodate a variety of items. In any case, there's no reason that your kitchen storage ever has to detract from the look of the room.

▶ **CUSTOMIZE TO IMPRESS.** Made-to-order cabinets like these are produced by a manufacturer, but they look like they were built in place by a master craftsman. Fine detailing, a unique finish, and a perfect fit set these handsome cabinets apart from prefab units. When you have the budget and are looking to redo an entire kitchen, custom cabinets can make the look.

▲ **SIMPLIFY WITH BAMBOO.** The eco-friendly bamboo cabinets shown here are typical, featuring uncomplicated lines in a frameless construction with understated graining. Bamboo is usually stained natural, although it takes colored stain well and can even be ebonized. You'll find slightly different grain patterns in different cabinets, but all are subtle and pretty. Best of all, the material is a grass, not actually a wood, so it grows fast and harvesting it is a sustainable practice.

◄ **EMPHASIZE GRAIN PATTERNS.** Basic raised-panel cabinets like these can certainly be painted or stained very dark, but staining them light not only keeps a small kitchen like this one light and feeling expansive, it also shows the wood grain at its best. Here, the honey-colored graining of the maple cabinets seems to almost shimmer, adding immeasurably to the look of the room. Every different wood has its own grain pattern, and you might even choose your cabinets based on the grain of the wood.

▲ **MIX MODERN STYLES.** Sleek black kitchen cabinetry often finds a natural partner in white surfaces and stainless-steel appliances, but style rules were meant to be broken. Here, wood front cabinets are mixed in with the black units, creating an intriguing look. What makes this design work is that the cabinets are all frameless and feature the same stainless steel handles. Common elements like those are a great way to marry different styles, colors, or finishes on cabinetry.

◄ **USE MIDRANGE WOOD TONES TO MODERATE DARKER SHADES.** The black counters and stove, along with deep, olive-green wall paint, make this small kitchen a bit closed in. Blonde or light wood tones in the cabinets might have jarringly contrasted the darker elements of the design, but the midrange cherry finish on these stylish cabinets effectively keeps things from being too visually heavy. Cabinet finishes are a great way to bend the kitchen design in one direction or another, because the cabinets usually cover quite a bit of visual surface area.

INTERMINGLE TO ADD POP. This small kitchen design was already a bit eclectic, with swirling metal tiles and island insets, modern fixtures, and steel countertops, so mixing dark and blonde cabinets is all part of the fun. The contrast between the two—with the darker base cabinets keeping the design firmly rooted and the blond Euro-style cabinets complementing the nearly white wood floor—sets up visual tension that successfully walks the fine line between balance and discord.

ANNOUNCE TRADITIONAL STYLE WITH RICH FINISHES. The deep brown stain on these cabinets—in tandem with the traditional hardware—leaves no doubt as to the design theme of this traditional kitchen. Marble counters and the unusual addition of an undermount apron sink dress up the room, but the cabinets are the foundation of the design and of the style. If you're looking to create a recognizable style in your kitchen, look first at the correct cabinet finish for the period or theme.

SAY MODERN WITH "SLAB" DOORS. Flat-front doors go high style when you create them from maple and finish them blonde, as was done for this kitchen. Wraparound twin island granite countertops and matching wall cabinets give this modern space a very sleek aspect and wonderfully light and clean feel. The oversized frameless cabinets are not only incredibly beautiful, they also allow maximum access to the interior space, making them quite useful as well.

KITCHEN CABINETS: REPLACE OR REFACE?

Sparkling new kitchen cabinets are eye-catching centerpieces in a kitchen. But they also represent a major cost, one that can easily run into six figures. Refacing existing cabinetry is a less-expensive option. The decision to reface or replace depends on the state of your current cabinets, the look you're after, and other factors.

Refacing involves removing and replacing doors, drawer fronts, and hardware, and cladding the exposed portions of existing cabinet boxes with panels that match the new doors. The three types of refacing materials are laminate, rigid thermofoil (RTF), and wood veneer. Laminates are plastic composites much like countertop laminates. They offer a wide range of colors and patterns, but are prone to delamination, wear, and chipping. RTF facing can be formed over surface relief elements and is available in a number of different appearances. Wood veneer is the facing of choice where you want a realistic wood appearance. The veneer is available in both softwood and hardwood appearances.

Refacing cabinets can save you half what you would have spent on replacements, but the decision will also rely on the existing cabinets. Much older cabinets may feature sturdy, solid-wood boxes. These are ideal foundations for refacing. But if cabinets are more recent versions crafted of MDF—or if the boxes are compromised in any way—they should be replaced. New cabinets may also make more sense if you're reconfiguring the layout of the kitchen.

Any cabinet refacing contractor should be licensed and insured. As in working with any trade professional, obtain the initial quote in writing, listing exactly the material to be used and the final price including installation and scheduling (the process takes two to four days). It's also wise to get at least three references and, if possible, check out those installations in person to see if the work meets your quality standards.

▶ **REPEAT INTERESTING FEATURES FOR MAX WOW.** The scalloped bottom edge on these good-looking cottage kitchen cabinets are copied in both the top and bottom units. This is a great way to reinforce the design theme and to decorate what are otherwise fairly plain cabinets. The detail on the bottom of these units adds just enough flair in the curvy profile to spruce up the look without corrupting the design style.

EMPHASIZE FINE POINTS FOR EXTRA FLAIR. These finely detailed cabinets have been finished with thin darker lines following the panel profile sections, which draws the eye to the incredible detail of the cabinet doors. The footed columns at each end of the cabinet run, and the matching dishwasher front, reinforce the reality that these are very high-end cabinets. A marble countertop is the perfect luxury addition to the sophisticated style of these units.

▶ **MATCH COUNTERTOP TO CABINETS.** Although you can choose a distinctive countertop material for your kitchen, it's easier to select cabinets and then match the countertop to the cabinets you've selected. Here, a perfect match is achieved between beige cabinets and a laminate countertop crafted to look like a travertine stone surface. The rough visual texture of the counter contrasts the smooth cabinet surface, but the colors are perfectly in sync—right down to the silver highlights in the counter that pick up on the silver cabinet pulls.

▽ **MIX IN WOOD.** For a truly alluring look, mix and match wood cabinet fronts with painted fronts, in the same kitchen design. The wood-fronted cabinets here set the island apart from the background wall, and add a lot to the look of the kitchen with the vibrant grain pattern. The island's cabinets also tie to the wood backsplash, unifying the entire kitchen design. A wonderful thing about wood fronts is they go with virtually any color of cabinet front, so mixing and matching is easy, even if you decide to change the color scheme.

▲ **COLOR CABINETS GREEN FOR TIMELESS STYLE.** Next to white, green is perhaps the favorite color for kitchen cabinets, and for good reason. The color carries with it associations of nature and can have a calming effect on a room that is often extremely busy in large household. A mid-range green such as this one—neither so bright that it strays into neon territory nor so somber that it dims the design—is ideal for a hue that will look good over time. This style of green with its modest black undertone is likely to look as good in five years as it does today.

◀ **INSTITUTE STATELY WITH GRAY.** For as long as people have been decorating houses, gray has been used for its connotations of authority, dignity, and solemnity. If you're creating a sophisticated, high-end kitchen style such as the one shown here, gray is a natural tone for the cabinetry. Use a darker gray to hide dirt, wear, and tear. Regardless of the gray you choose, though, don't forget the details like the simple and elegant handles and pulls on these cabinets. You can also use glass fronts to provide some sparkle to an otherwise staid look.

▲ **CREATE A CLEAN AIRY FEEL WITH BRIGHT WHITE.** A pure white, like the shade used on these cabinets, makes for an upbeat feel in the kitchen. It also pretty much shouts cleanliness. A bank of glass cabinet doors is the perfect partner for white cabinets, because the interiors are usually white, and the glass adds sparkle to the bright surface of the cabinets. Small details, like the artfully designed dual faucets, provide even more visual interest. It's a sharp look that works well across kitchen design styles.

▲ **ACCENT FRAMELESS CABINETS WITH GLASS.** A sleek contemporary kitchen like this one is all about subtle style. Solid colors, reflective surfaces, and simple straight lines all create an impressive look, but also one that can tend toward the sedate. Add a little spark to the design with a couple of accent cabinet fronts, and you create the opportunity to show off vases, attractive dinnerware, and other visually interesting items. Use what's in the cabinet to display a few curves or a splash of color to contrast the rest of the design.

▲ **REFLECT A SMALL REALITY, SO THAT IT APPEARS LARGER.** Using mirrors to make a small room seem much larger is an effective design strategy that's been used almost as long as people have been decorating homes. It can be just as effective in the kitchen as it is in other rooms, especially if you replace cabinet glass inserts with mirrored panels. The effect is glamorous, introducing extra brilliance and visually expanding the room—essential in a tiny kitchen like this.

▶ **RETAIN TRADITIONAL STYLE WITH ISOLATED GLASS FRONTS.**
Glass fronts in all the upper cabinets in this kitchen would
have interrupted the semiformal look and drawn attention
away from the rest of the design details. Instead, by using
glass for only the topmost cabinet sections, the designer
created display spaces that accent rather than overwhelm the
design. This treatment is common in more formal kitchens,
and custom cabinet manufacturers, such as the company
that made these units, offer divided cabinets with glassed-in
sections like these as part of their lineup.

▼ **CREATE A CLASSIC LOOK WITH GRAY AND WHITE.** White
cabinets in this kitchen would have made the space too
sterile and blindingly bright. The elegant gray cabinets not
only moderate the white background, but they also lend a
sophisticated look to the whole space. Accented with chrome
pulls and sandwiched between bright white surfaces and
an ebony floor, the gray seems clean and visually pleasing.
By going with such a classic combo, the homeowner has
ensured that the kitchen design won't get tired or fade like a
trendier look might have.

▲ **CONSIDER OUTSIDE-FACING CABINETS TO MAKE THE MOST OF WHAT WOULD OTHERWISE BE DEAD SPACE.** This handsome suite of cabinets includes a set on the outside of the sink. Although the cabinets are shallow to allow for the plumbing on the other side of the counter, they are perfect for placemats and tableware that will see use on the adjacent kitchen table.

◄ **VISUALLY ORGANIZE THE KITCHEN THROUGH AN ENLIGHTENED PLACEMENT OF CABINETS AND SHELVES.** The location of the shelves in this kitchen allow much more freedom of movement and light penetration around the cooktop, and the placement of trays of dinnerware in a far, glass-fronted cabinet makes sense because these items will be used less frequently than the foodstuffs stored in the cabinets nearest the island and the ovens.

▶ **LET SIMPLICITY SERVE WHEN THE KITCHEN CALLS FOR IT.**
The cabinets in this modest kitchen don't call attention to
themselves and they don't need to. The kitchen—and the
cabinets—are all about understated elegance, with restrained
features such as the under-cabinet shelves and curving toe
kicks that add style without going over the top. The look of
this kitchen and its storage will never grow old.

▼ **BLEND CABINET FRONT STYLES TO MAXIMIZE STORAGE
POTENTIAL AND GIVE THE KITCHEN ADDED FLAIR.** The suite
of cabinets here includes a mix of raised-panel (gray) and
inset-panel (cream) cabinets, with complementary styles and
matching pulls and handles. The suite includes elegant glass-
fronted units, plate-holder shelves, and open storage areas.
The combinations provide a place for everything that needs
to be stored, and visual excitement and variety.

▲ **OPEN UP A CRAMPED KITCHEN WITH GLASS ON BOTH SIDES OF A CABINET.** This small cottage kitchen needs to maintain as much flow as possible to keep the space from becoming visibly closed in and claustrophobic. Using glass on both sides of the pass-through upper cabinets allows for light to transmit deep into the kitchen and provides a lovely visual of stacked dinnerware and attractive glassware. This also prevents the back of the cabinets from facing out or facing into the kitchen, something that would detract from any kitchen design.

MAKE YOUR KITCHEN ACCESSIBLE.

Accessibility design involves creating kitchens with features that conform to the Americans with Disabilities Act and the best standards and practices of universal design. The idea is to make the whole space accessible to the disabled, elderly, and infirm who have trouble reaching high spaces, opening stiff doors, and performing other tasks the rest of us take for granted. The manufacturer of these cabinets, Freedom Lift Systems, crafts them to mount on motorized columns so that the shelves inside can be raised and lowered at the push of a button. They also produce countertops that can be raised and lowered, and base cabinet units with shelves that telescope out on mechanical arms. As with most accessible design cabinetry and countertops, these are offered in a selection of different finishes and styles.

▶ **ADAPT SPECIALIZED STORAGE TO YOUR NEEDS.** Got a dog and want to avoid the mess of dog food bags spilling all over? Use a pull-out cabinet insert such as the one shown here to collect large amounts of dog food and a few doggie treats. This double-pail feature could be used for recyclables or garbage just as easily as it serves as pet food storage. That's why cabinet features like this are incredibly useful and adaptable in any kitchen.

▲ **EXPLOIT SKINNY SPACES.** Pull-out shelving custom sized for items such as spice jars, tins, or bottles are incredibly handy and make keeping your kitchen organized a breeze. These features are usually mounted with top and bottom slides that make the drawer easy to move out and in with a touch. The best thing is that they make great use of areas that would have otherwise been dead space. You'll even find full-height versions that can essentially serve as tall, skinny pantries!

◀ **PERFECTLY PLACED PULL-OUT SPICE ORGANIZERS.** A custom spice rack like this is one of the nicest specialty storage features you can order from a custom cabinet manufacturer. Just be sure, though, that you can locate the spice rack close to a prep or cooking area. The convenience of the metal-slide-mounted feature will be somewhat negated if you have to walk across the room to get to the spices. Storage feature location should always be carefully thought out, to ensure these features are as convenient as possible.

▲ **TRY TRAYS FOR STORAGE FLEXIBILITY.** Tray drawer organizers can be excellent for storing odd-shaped containers that might not fit comfortably in a plain drawer or in other organizers. The glass jars in this drawer would otherwise fall over if not sequestered in their own trays, and the trays could just as easily be used to hold groups of utensils.

◀ **ADD A PULLOUT CUTTING BOARD.** It doesn't matter if you're an avid foodie or just a weeknight hurry-up cook, cutting boards are essential additions to the kitchen. A pull-out hardwood cutting board like this one will add little expense to your custom cabinets, but will provide tons of convenience and ease when it comes to preparing meals. You can choose to add a cutting board right over a drawer, as shown here, or opt to place it over a tall base cabinet. Either way, use hardwood for the longest-lasting surface.

◀ **DESIGN TO ORGANIZE.** When choosing kitchen cabinets and drawers, look for custom features that will make your life easier and keep your kitchen in order. Simple drawer organizers like these can be an amazing convenience and will help you ensure that everything in your kitchen has a place close to where the utensil, textile, or dishware will be used.

▼ **LOCATE DRAWERS WHERE THEY'LL HAVE THE GREATEST IMPACT.** Cooktop drawers are incredibly useful because they place what you need right where you'll use it. Here, a shallow utensil and flatware drawer sits right under the gas cooktop, with a deeper, larger pot drawer on the bottom (where the weightier items should naturally go). The drawers make cooking and working around the cooktop much easier and more convenient.

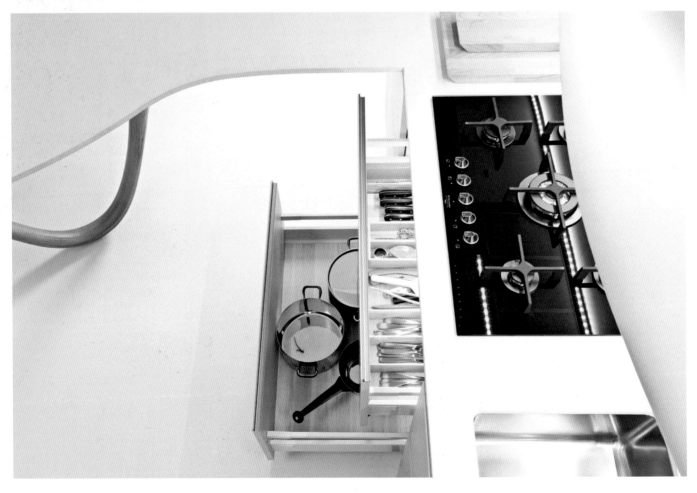

▲ **MAKE ACCESS EASY WITH EXPOSED DRAWERS.** The large, deep pullout drawers in this kitchen island are just the thing to keep a wealth of pots and pans at the ready, right where they'll be used. Using drawers rather than a cabinet for this storage is a wise decision. The drawers circumvent the need to reach and they help keep the pots and pans organized. The same manufacturer that produced the cabinets in the rest of the kitchen—including the units in this island—produced the pull-out drawers. Most large cabinet manufacturers provide one-stop shopping by offering a full complement of storage options.

▲ **WEAVE YOUR WINE INTO YOUR CABINETRY.** Wine bottles should be stored laying on their sides and kept secure from anywhere the bottles might be knocked over and broken. Storing wine above a cabinet is ideal, and is also a lovely decorative feature that makes any kitchen look sophisticated. The wine here is stored in a manufactured cabinet unit with room for glassware in glass-fronted cabinets below. The unit was installed in a kitchen alcove that is used as a minibar area. This is an example of focusing the design of one area in the kitchen on one aspect of cooking and dining—a strategy that can work throughout the kitchen.

◄ **SELECT CABINET FEATURES THAT SUIT YOUR LIFE.** Do you keep cleaning products and lots of other materials under the sink? Then you might benefit from this specialized undersink cabinet. It has a specially formulated polymer base that won't be damaged by spills. A ridged surface ensures that everything stored under the sink is kept slightly above any moisture that might collect, and the entire cabinet box interior is extremely cleanable. Proprietary innovations like this can make your kitchen much more efficient, depending on how and where you want to store everything in the room.

▲ **USE DIVIDERS IN LARGE DRAWERS AS WELL AS SMALL.** Although drawer dividers are most common for flatware and similar small-drawer items, adding dividers to larger drawers is also a great way to keep things in order. Incorporate pockets of different sizes and shapes to create the most usable space possible. Many dividers are also adjustable, giving you even more control over what you store where.

TIPS

FREESTANDING CABINET TIPS

Freestanding kitchen cabinets are a wonderful option for contemporary or European-style kitchens. The cabinets take less time and effort to install than standard wall-mounted cabinets, and they are easier to reconfigure in the event you change the layout of the kitchen. Follow these guidelines when purchasing freestanding cabinets:

• Always carefully unpack cartons and immediately check the parts included against the parts list.

• Use painter's tape to attach hardware packets and instructions to their respective cabinet parts or sections.

• If you're assembling the cabinets in a garage or workspace separate from the kitchen, make sure you have a wide enough means of access to move the assembled unit into the kitchen.

• Double check that the correct side of the cabinet back faces into the cabinet.

• Ensure that any drawers are right side up before drilling handle holes.

• Use a helper whenever possible to avoid damaging cabinet panels by dropping or dragging them.

◄ **ARRANGE SHELVES AS A COMPOSITION ON A STANDOUT WALL SURFACE.** Stone tiles serve as the perfect foil for a set of wood floating shelves. Not only is the wall stunning in its own right, but it gives the shelves pronounced visual depth that showcases the reclaimed wood and the serving ware stored on the shelves.

◀ **IF YOU HAVE IT, FLAUNT IT!**
Alcove shelving is a wonderful alternative to installing cabinets. Alcoves lend themselves to shelves because shelves show the architecture to better advantage than a set of cabinets would. Cabinets would also be more difficult to install in the limited space of an alcove like this one. If you choose significant shelving area, like the space shown here, use it for the best-looking dinnerware, serving pieces, or glassware you own. The alcove becomes a kind of visual frame, drawing attention to whatever you put on the shelves. In this kitchen, the crisp white shelves work perfectly with the tiled backsplash and the dark tiles crafted to look like wood flooring.

▲ **DIVIDE ROOMS WITH OPEN SHELVING.** Open shelving allows for the free flow of air and light, and gives a kitchen a more informal look. The open shelves in this room are used for display pieces, but could just as easily hold cookbooks, or cookware—anything that looks attractive from both sides. Even though you can see through shelves like this, they create a vivid visual border that helps define different areas in an open floor plan, such as the kitchen and dining area in this house.

▲ **COMBINE SHELVES AND CABINETS FOR CONTEMPORARY BLISS.** The unique storage unit lining one wall of this super-cool space has a sliding front. Shelves on either side are used to display attractive bowls and vessels, while the center section is concealed behind the door. The homeowner has the option of changing the look and sliding the door over either end to expose the middle section. It's a very contemporary feature and also a design highlight.

◁ **CHOOSE A TRADITIONAL POT RACK FOR EASIER COOKING.** A basic, sturdy, over-island pot rack like the one shown here is not only an interesting addition to any kitchen design, but it is also makes pots and pans more accessible. Put the rack over a prep area or cooktop, and it's easy to grab the pot you need in a flash. This also frees up cabinet space that would have been poorly optimized to store awkwardly shaped cookware.

▲ **MIX SHELVES FOR A FUNKY AND FRESH LOOK.** Wood shelves intermingle with stainless steel platforms in this upbeat kitchen with lime green walls. It's a lively look that brings fun to the design, and keeps utensils, plates, and more right at hand. Blonde wood goes especially well with stainless steel, creating a Euro-look that remains novel and airy long after it is installed.

◁ **USE AN UNUSUAL POT RACK AS A VISUAL.** Hanging pot racks come in all kinds of metals (and some woods), including high-gloss chrome, brushed nickel, and the incredibly distinctive copper shown here. It's a wonderful addition to a kitchen—especially if you're hanging copper pots or pans. The look works best with lighter wood cabinets or those that are finished in a stain that has red tones in it.

PICK A MULTIPURPOSE RACK. Dual-use fixtures are the most efficient you can buy, and this is one of the best. Combining task lighting and a full-fledged pot rack, this overhead fixture couldn't be handier. It's also attractive in its own right, with edging that matches the cabinetry and abundant LED lighting perfect for tasks requiring exacting precision and safety.

◀ **MAKE USE OF DEAD WALL SPACE.**
Hanging storage bars come in a
range of lengths, so that you can
use the length that best suits your
available space. But when you have
an open wall that begs for some
ornamentation, fill it with the happy
clutter of utensils and cookware by
using the longest bars you can find.
Be sure to position the bars for easy
access—eye level for heavier or larger
objects, and lower down for lighter
utensils and cookware.

▲ **EXPLOIT BACKSPLASH WALL SPACE.** You'll find completely integrated, all-in-one, wall-mounted hanging systems available
from many different kitchen supply and general home retail stores. These are ideal for dressing up a large backsplash area,
such as the stunningly glass-tiled surface in this kitchen. The systems include configurations with shelves, hanging bars,
matching S hooks, and simple-to-install brackets. The look is neat and trim, and rather sleek as well. As this kitchen illustrates,
it's a beautiful way to get a cooking area in order.

BREATHTAKING APPLIANCES

Striking Refrigerators

Dynamic Dishwashers
& Compactors

Fascinating Ovens, Cooktops
& Ranges

Wonderful Wine Refrigerators

Eye-Catching Vent Hoods

Appliances are often the odd men out in a kitchen design. The function of any kitchen appliance—small or large—is so crucial that the aesthetic considerations take a back seat. If you've been pining for that restaurant-quality six-burner gas stove, you probably aren't concerned about the stainless-steel front and how it fits into the greater scheme of your kitchen's look.

But appliance appearance is worthy of consideration. For the most part, these are rather large visuals in a kitchen. Your kitchen will usually feature a suite of appliances that create visual anchors around the room. They can have more impact than most homeowners realize.

That's why the larger appliances in the kitchen have traditionally been offered in stainless steel, black, and white. With new advances in stainless steel finishes that don't show fingerprints, streaks, or smudges, that has once again become the appliance

material of choice. The look fits with most kitchen designs and is rather timeless, so that a stainless-steel appliance will complement colors and textures in the space even as you update the kitchen over time.

However, the high-end trend toward concealing refrigerators and dishwashers behind panels that match surrounding cabinetry continues. This is a lovely way of integrating these essential kitchen players in a way that makes them just part of the design. It also gives the flexibility of changing the face of appliances whenever you choose to change the face of your cabinets.

Regardless of whatever look you choose, keep in mind that appliances are the hardest-working members of your kitchen design and the most crucial pieces in determining how easy it is to work in the space. In any kitchen redesign, always consider appliance positioning first, then adapt other elements around them.

▶ **GO STAINLESS STEEL WITH GRAY.** A stainless steel look is naturally suited to a gray color scheme. The stately deep gray in this kitchen is kept from becoming overly dark by bright white surfaces, and the reflective nature of the stainless steel also amplifies the light in the space. It's an overall handsome look, where the appliances actually become active design features as much as workhorses.

COCOON YOUR REFRIGERATOR.
Containing a refrigerator in a cavity is a common practice that hides the featureless sides of the unit and focuses attention on the well-designed face. This technique is especially effective when you're working with high-end, pro-quality units like the side-by-side freezer and refrigerator here, complemented by a wine refrigerator with door window. An alcove or setback of any sort becomes a frame to showcase gorgeous appliances like this.

BE SURE THE INSIDE OF A FRIDGE WORKS AS WELL AS THE OUTSIDE. You can find many different refrigerators with decorative panels to match cabinetry, as with the wood fronts on this unit. But while the look of your refrigerator has a big impact on the room's design, you also want to make sure that the refrigerator you buy accommodates what you need to store. This over-and-under model features a bottom drawer set up to accommodate common sizes of beverages and other specific food containers.

TIPS

REFRIGERATOR CARE

Refrigerators aren't cheap. The same is true of refrigerator repairs. The good news is that a few simple steps can ensure a long, trouble-free life for your refrigerator, and can help save you energy costs over the long haul.

- **KEEP COILS DIRT-FREE.** Condenser coils are essential to the efficient operation of any refrigerator. Located on the back of the refrigerator, or under a grill at the bottom front, the coils carry the chemical refrigerant, releasing heat carried from the interior of the refrigerator. Dirty coils covered with debris like pet hair not only operate less efficiently (causing the unit to use more electricity), but they also lead to breakdowns. Pros recommend cleaning the coils twice a year, but the frequency really depends on how busy your kitchen is. Make it a monthly task and you'll probably never experience a coil-related problem.

- **CLEAN THE CONDENSER FAN.** If your coils are on the back of the unit, you don't have a fan. But if they are on the front, under a grill, a condenser fan pulls air in over the coils to disperse heat. Dirt, dust, pet hair, or other debris can clog the fan. A quick wipe down and a cleaning using a brush attachment on a vacuum will ensure efficient operation. Use the opportunity to clean out the drip pan. Most refrigerators include a diagram showing the location of these parts—it may be on the back of the unit or behind the front grill.

- **DOOR-GASKET HYGIENE.** The expandable gasket around the door is the last line of defense against energy waste. A dirty gasket can create an incomplete seal, allowing cold air to leak out of the refrigerator, causing the compressor to work overtime, and costing you hard-earned cash. Cleaning the gasket couldn't be easier. Mix warm water with a squirt or two of dish soap and wipe down the entire gasket. Be sure to remove obvious sticky spots such as dried juice splashes, and carefully clean inside the creases. Wipe dry with a clean towel and dust the gasket with a cloth coated in talcum powder.

- **CLEAR DRIP OPENINGS AND VENTS.** The vents inside your refrigerator allow for proper air circulation and energy-efficient operation. They should be kept free of any blockage. Drip openings drain condensation and water from defrost cycles down to the drip pan at the bottom of the refrigerator. The drip openings must be kept unobstructed for proper refrigerator operation. Check your refrigerator's manual for the location and the manufacturer's recommended method of cleaning drip tubes.

▶ **CUSTOMIZE FOR A CHIC UNIQUE LOOK.** If you've set a high bar for your kitchen design, you might want to consider a totally custom installation like the one shown here. These mirror side-by-side units are a freezer on one side with a refrigerator on the other. Both are clad in the same wood paneling that covers the wall, with custom-made vent openings and handles in the same wood. This kind of detailing on an appliance is admittedly pricey, but it's also incredibly stunning and can be a jaw-dropping feature in any kitchen.

▽ **BLEND YOUR REFRIGERATOR INTO THE ROOM.** Appliance manufacturers now offer, as part of their upscale lines, the ability to match refrigerator fronts to existing cabinetry. This allows you to create a nearly seamless design that exploits beautiful surfaces like the heavily grained wood fronts in this kitchen. This particular model of refrigerator includes a window, adding to the allure and giving you a peek inside the refrigerator without having to open the door (which saves precious energy and lowers your monthly bill).

◀ **HIDE A DISHWASHER.** As with refrigerators, dishwasher manufacturers offer customized front panels to match the look of kitchen cabinets. This can help you create a seamless appearance along a row of base cabinets, especially those with handsome or uniquely finished doors. Less expensive dishwashers often come with multiple front panels that can be swapped out. Although these won't match your existing cabinetry exactly, they do allow you to change the look and find one that best suits your kitchen design.

▼ **FOR A CLEAN, FRESH LOOK.** Sometimes, the appliance's façade works just fine in the design. In a bank of bright white cabinets, a stainless steel dishwasher looks right at home. The surface is not only bright and reflective, it is also easy to keep clean. And keep in mind that stainless steel appliance fronts are quickly becoming a classic and traditional look. Look for brushed or textured stainless steel if you have a lot of children in your house and you want to spend less time cleaning fingerprints off your appliances.

▲ **HIDE CONTROLS WHEN POSSIBLE.** A grid of controls on the front of a dishwasher usually detracts from the look of the unit and makes it impossible to dress up the façade with any kind of special or custom panel. The better options are top-mounted controls, along the lip or edge of the unit. Many of today's more upscale appliances feature these kind of hidden controls, which leads to a much cleaner look in the kitchen. If you're going upscale with your design, it's a good idea to consider hidden controls.

◀ **POSITION A COMPACTOR WHERE IT LOOKS BEST.** A trash compactor doesn't necessarily need to be in any one place in the kitchen (as opposed to a dishwasher that is normally placed right next to the sink). That's why you should look for a place to put it that makes the most visual sense. Positioned on the inside wall of a large island, a trash compactor is still conveniently at hand, but largely invisible to anyone but the cook. The homeowner here has placed the compactor in a run of standard-sized cabinets—the same size as the trash compactor. This creates a uniform visual rhythm that is pleasing to the eye, even though the compactor presents a different finish.

▶ **BLEND AN INDUCTION RANGE INTO THE COUNTER.** This stainless steel induction cooktop reads as a blank reflective surface, matching the surface of the stainless steel countertops on either side. The combination creates a high-tech look that intimates serious cooking. This type of treatment takes some planning because the cooktop is nearly on level with the countertops. The surrounding darker surfaces emphasize the illusion.

◀ **KEEP THE RANGE CLOSE TO THE CORNER.** Whenever possible, locate the range in a compact triangle with the prep area and refrigerator. The location of this range is just about perfect. Countertops on either side allow for handy surfaces to keep ingredients going into pots, and the sink is just a step away from the cooktop, making cleanup a breeze. You can't always determine where the appliances will go, but when you can, make sure the placement is effective for ease of use.

ADD MEGA CONVENIENCE WITH A BUILT-IN WARMING DRAWER. Cooktops are the height of luxury for an avid cook, but if you want to make the cooktop even more useful, install a warming drawer like this one, right below the cooktop. It's almost as easy as installing a cabinet drawer, although it does require wiring into the cooktop circuit. But with a little effort, you can keep food warm while you finish preparing that perfect meal for your next dinner party. Put the drawer behind a front that matches the surrounding cabinets to finish the feature in high style.

GROUP RANGES AND MICROWAVES. The reality is that microwaves are often used in conjunction with a range—say, to melt a key ingredient before it is added to a pot or pan. So it only makes sense to position them in close proximity. The accepted practice, where possible, is to mount the microwave right over the range. This entails a fan that sucks fumes from the cooktop back behind the microwave, but that's easy enough to have installed. When combining appliances in an arrangement like this, it works best if each has the same finish.

▲ **MAKE A HIGH-END RANGE A DESIGN CENTERPIECE.** If you are spending the money and making the commitment to a restaurant-quality appliance like this, it only makes sense to shine the design spotlight on the unit. Here, the homeowner has positioned the range in front of an easy-to-clean and simply spectacular wall clad in stainless steel. A crowded pot rack overhead adds to the impression of a professional's kitchen, and the entire look is impressive and arresting.

◀ **WALL MOUNT FOR A TRIM LOOK AND SUPER CONVENIENCE.** This wall-mount installation includes, from top to bottom, a microwave, oven, and warming drawer. The look is chic, with all the appliances contained in a single column topped by a handy cabinet. Notice the thick, sturdy handles that guarantee a sure grip on the doors, and high-tech controls that give the look some serious foodie cred. Stacking appliances like this is a great way to conserve space and create a cooking and baking center point in the kitchen.

▼ **CLUSTER KEY APPLIANCES FOR MAXIMUM EFFICIENCY.** This is especially important in a small kitchen such as this. The placement of the range, refrigerator, and sink/dishwasher creates a tight work triangle that saves steps, time, and frustration and makes best use of three high-end appliances. Work lighting over each of the appliances makes them easier to use and highlights the stainless steel finish.

INJECT STYLE WITH A HEAVY-DUTY ELECTRIC RANGE. Electric ranges used to be the ugly sister in the kitchen, an also-ran to the restaurant styling of gas units. Not anymore. This high-end electric range includes the easy-to-grasp control knobs, sturdy feet, and rock solid construction you'd expect in a top-shelf gas unit. The looks are only one part of the equation; newer electric ranges are super quick to heat up and more exacting than ever in temperature ranges. If your current unit leads to spoiled meals, it may be time to upgrade your style and your cooking capacity.

ADD A HANDSOME DOUBLE-DUTY WORKHORSE. The classic, sturdy gas-range look captured in the styling of this stunning unit is just part of the appliance's appeal. It's actually an efficient electric convection oven topped by a gourmet gas cooktop. These days, manufacturers not only offer an amazing array of looks for their appliances, they also provide all the functionality you could ask for.

PULL OUT THE STOPS WHEN COOKING IS YOUR LIFE. For a busy kitchen, or if you are just a chef-quality home cook, consider going big with a fully featured luxury gas range like the one shown here. Including a grill, six burners, and a double oven, this is serious cooking power for the serious cook. But it's also true eye candy, with an unusual matte black finish that matches both the hood and the other appliances in the kitchen. The finish plays perfectly against the yellow in the blonde cabinet finishes. You couldn't ask for a more stunning look in the kitchen.

MARRY GAS BURNERS AND STONE SURFACES. The appeal of iron grates set against a natural stone background is simply undeniable. Here, the intricate stone mosaic tile backsplash makes the sleek stainless steel pop, and the marble surfaces give the cooktop the perfect stage. This particular unit sports chunky red controls that are easy to use and provide a fun splash of color for the eye. As part of a suite of luxury stainless steel appliances, it completes a jaw-dropping kitchen design full of appealing natural materials that present a mix of textural effects.

▲ **MAKE A SECONDARY SINK AREA SPECIAL WITH A WINE REFRIGERATOR.** This small alcove is tiled in stunning style with glass mosaics that make the space sparkle. It calls for special appliances that can create something more than a bar sink area. A blue-lit wine refrigerator adds a bit of color and lot of convenience to the drinks zone. The stainless steel styling complements the crisp tile and exposed storage, and although it's modest in size, the refrigerator holds a good number of bottles—as many as any party might call for.

▶ **TURN YOUR ISLAND INTO A BEVERAGE CENTER.** The bookended refrigerators on this island provide a lot of refreshment as well as interesting visuals. The front doors match the oversized drawer fronts, and a wine refrigerator keeps vintage whites at the ready for any party (or just a stylish weeknight dinner). Slide-out drawers provide easy access to the bottles, and hidden controls give you the ability to adjust the temperature as desired. Luxury porcelain floor tile with a surprisingly convincing wood look completes a very pretty picture.

INDULGE YOUR PASSION WITH A FULL-SIZE WINE REFRIGERATOR. This unit features a top vent and interior-mounted temperature controls that leave the front glass door plain and elegant, with a wood frame that matches the surrounding cabinetry. Interior lights make it easy to find the bottle you're looking for without opening the door, and slide out trays provide effort-free accessibility to your wine collection. It's the height of luxury and convenience in wine storage and a tremendously sophisticated look.

Eye-Catching Vent Hoods

● ○ ○ ○ ○ ○

▽ **GET CURVY FOR SEDUCTIVE APPEAL.** Curved range hoods are less common than straight-line models, which makes them an unusual look in a contemporary kitchen. But they also bring a bit of drama and flair to kitchen designs featuring an abundance of straight lines and flat surfaces, such as this sleek space. Add glass ledges like those on this hood, and the hood becomes a truly distinctive design element.

▲ **ADD HANGERS FOR USABILITY AND PANACHE.** The utensil hangers included on this hood are just one of several accessories that can be added to this cooktop hood. Buy one with directional lighting to illuminate different parts of the cooking area, or choose a hood with integral shelves to add attractive storage right near where you do your cooking.

◀ **INJECT WHIMSY WITH A CLAD HOOD.** This country kitchen features stunning cabinetry that's true to style and understated, just as the countertops and walls are. But the nearly bell-shaped range hood is not only oddly proportioned, it's coated in a bright white enamel with metal strips outlining the shape. It's an interesting decorative element that if styled more traditionally, would have melted into the background. As it is, it brings a smile to the face of any visitor.

OVEN MAINTENANCE

Keeping your oven up to snuff isn't just a matter of ensuring it lasts as long as possible. A properly maintained oven will heat food uniformly so that cooking is easier and more predictable, and it is also less likely to produce unpleasant smells and smoke.

- **CLEANING THE INTERIOR.** Although many cooks avoid it, the inside of a regularly used oven should be cleaned every few months. Older ovens may require a good scrubbing (heat a pan of water in the oven for 30 minutes on 400 degrees Fahrenheit to loosen stubborn food particles), but most modern units have a self-cleaning feature. However, only use the self-cleaning setting after you've read the manufacturer's instructions. Don't leave the house while the oven is in self-cleaning mode, and open a window and use the hood fan to alleviate some of the heat and fumes produced by the process. Once the cycle is finished, allow the stove to cool down before using it.

- **DEGRIMING GAS-STOVE GRATES.** Spray the grates with oven cleaner and put them in a sealed plastic bag for one hour. All they'll need after that is a mild scrubbing to look like new.

- **CLEAN ELECTRIC BURNERS.** For simple messes, turn the burners on high and leave them for 15 minutes. If they need deeper cleaner, detach them from the controller and scrub with a scrubber sponge moistened with hot water and dish soap. Rinse and allow the burner to dry completely before plugging it back into the controller.

- **ELECTRIC GLASS TOPS.** Whether it's the burners or the control panel, range glass tops should be cleaned with the mildest glass cleaner you can find, used according to the manufacturer's directions. The most common way to clean these is with a clean, lint-free cloth and wipe away any food residue.

- **KNOBS.** Never spray cleaner underneath oven control knobs; you can short out the electrical system. Instead, soak knobs in a solution of hot water and dishwashing soap for up to an hour.

▲ **DOMINATE A KITCHEN DESIGN WITH A DISTINCTIVE, METAL-WORKED HOOD.** This one-of-kind hood and duct were hand crafted out of burnished sheet metal. The craftsmanship is apparent and the sheer visual power overwhelms the function of the hood, as the hood becomes the design centerpiece in the room. Keep in mind that this sort of custom creation can be pricey, but the visual effect is usually well worth the expense.

▶ **USE DUCTWORK FOR DRAMA.** Kitchen hoods often vent directly through a wall or through a drywall or cabinet column, meaning that the ductwork is hidden. But in a modern or sleek contemporary design that is all angles and lines, the ductwork itself can become something of an impressive design element. This minimal kitchen features breathtaking vaulted ceilings and a sweeping wall of windows, both of which are perfectly complemented by a dramatically flared hood cowl topped by a visually substantial duct column.

▶ **SURPRISE THE EYE WITH SHINY.**
This eclectic kitchen was the perfect place to change up the look of the oversized hood, and what better way than to use a totally unconventional finish? The glossy surface of the polished metal hood adds some brightness to an otherwise dark room design, balancing the gorgeous dark wood island and cabinets. It also accentuates the shape and form of the hood, helping it visually pop off the wall. Changing the conventional can often bring a surprising freshness to kitchen designs.

▲ **CENTRALIZE DESIGN FOCUS AROUND A CEILING-MOUNTED HOOD.** Hanging range hoods require a great deal of planning, but usually give you the chance to customize the kitchen's layout. Here, the layout is logically arranged, with the prep, storage, and clean-up on one side, the cooking area anchored by a handsome overhead hood in the middle, and the eating and relaxing section on the near side. It's a thoughtful layout, and the range hood is both an attractive addition and one that helps clearly define the separation between kitchen areas.

FRAME A SUBSTANTIAL HOOD. It's not like this hood lacks for drama, but framing it with a showcase tiled alcove makes it stand out even more. The hood is part of a stainless-steel ensemble that includes a restaurant-quality stove, stainless-steel shelves, and matching pot-filler faucet (along with the stainless steel utensil holder and utensils). The look is clean, but extremely high-end and luxurious. The abundance of stainless steel is like a thread that runs through the kitchen design, unifying it.

SAY IT PROUD. Sometimes, it's best to use the appropriate range hood without adornment, special treatments, or concealment. This is a handsome, sturdy, high-quality hood that looks great against a tiled wall. The natural wood textures, stone, and glass all around it complement the look of the stainless steel, and the hood's simple, crisp lines do justice to the busy patterns in the space. It was a wise choice not to try to dress up this already upscale appliance.

BLOCK IT OUT. The truth is, vent hoods come in all shapes and sizes, including the block-shaped self-contained unit in this kitchen. Although the vent hood calls little attention to itself, it is perfectly in keeping with the theme of the kitchen and the linear design style. The unique hood echoes the shapes of the custom cabinetry unit surrounding the range, and the distinctive U-shaped quartz island. It's a perfect blending of subtle form and function.

◄ **MATCH YOUR HOOD TO THE CABINETS FOR A COMPLETELY UNIFIED LOOK.** The modest vent hood in this kitchen has been clad in a veneer that matches the top and bottom cabinetry. It's a truly seamless look masking a feature that can sometimes be the odd player out in a darker design such as this. Materials are available to clad a vent hood to match just about any cabinet surface.

▼ **CRAFT AN OPULENT VENT HOOD ENCLOSURE TO MAKE A DESIGN CENTERPIECE OUT OF A FUNCTIONAL FEATURE.** The arched soffit and marble roof tiled around this restaurant-quality range's hood combines with the detailed marble backsplash wall to create a picture of luxury surrounding a high-performance kitchen appliance. Whenever possible, surround top-of-line appliances and fixtures with similarly luxurious surface materials.

BEAUTIFUL FIXTURES

Fashion-Forward Faucets

Swanky Sinks

They might seem like small pieces of a much bigger picture, but a faucet and sink can make an indelible impression on any kitchen design. Like a refrigerator or lighting fixture, every true kitchen must have at least one sink and faucet. But that doesn't mean you have to limit yourself; larger kitchens often do well with a standard sink and faucet, and a second, smaller prep sink on an island or a long prep countertop. Either way, both sink and faucet are your chance to embellish the look of the kitchen and make working in the room a lot easier. There's just no getting around the fact that no matter how good the duo look, the sink-faucet combo is the center of all kitchen clean up.

The faucet is naturally going to be the more high-profile member of that duo. Faucets are like jewelry for the kitchen,

and manufacturers have responded to the ever-growing hunger for new looks by producing faucets in an astounding number of finishes. You can find models in chrome, brushed nickel, stainless steel, enameled and plastic colors, antiqued bronze and iron, and more. The faucet's finish is naturally related to the form, and the form is indicative of the overall design style, from retro to country to modern.

Sinks have also come a long way from the simple choice of yesteryear between enameled white and stainless steel. These days, you'll find sinks in black, white, and colors as well as the continually popular stainless steel. On the low end, you can buy an acrylic sink in a range of colors, but you'll need to baby it because the material is easy to scratch and will melt under high

▶ **MATCH A DUOTONE FAUCET TO THE SINK FOR MAXIMUM VISUAL IMPACT.** Two-tone faucets are becoming increasingly popular thanks to the distinctive look. The curvy, tree-branch shape of this one is alluring all by itself, but even more so with splashes of gray on the body and faucet tip. Using a sink in the exact same color ties the look together and doubles the impact of the faucet alone.

◁ **ADORN WITH GRACE.** If you're willing to spend a bit more on your faucet, you can add visual poetry to a modern or contemporary kitchen with a sleek modern faucet. As this example shows, the latest faucets are the height of style and feature an exceptional interpretation of the classic gooseneck arch. A block lever looks almost seamless with the faucet body when turned off, and is part of a sophisticated appearance that can help define a clean modern aesthetic.

heat. Stainless steel is a durable choice with a look that fits into just about any kitchen style. Go with a thicker gauge to ensure longevity. Solid-surface sinks can be fabricated right into a solid-surface countertop and the color goes all the way through, so scratches aren't a problem. Enameled cast iron remains popular as well, because the sink will take a lot of abuse (although you do have to keep an eye out for chipping).

The finish is only one side of the sinks' coin. You'll also be choosing between one, two, or three bowls, as well as picking a mounting style. Sinks can be self-rimming (also known as top mount), with a lip that rests on top of the counter. Or you can choose an undermount sink, which makes for easy cleanup but

requires a countertop that can be fabricated with an exposed inside edge. Apron-front sinks are yet another version, with a front face that is completely exposed. These are impressive kitchen additions that contain abundant room in a single bowl for cleaning larger pots and pans.

No matter what style, shape, or color you're considering, you'll want to pick your faucet and sink at the same time. Once installed, they become lifelong visual and working partners. Choose carefully, and you'll make your kitchen more efficient, more pleasant to work in, and a space that sparkles during cleanup and at other times as well.

GO FOR THE GOLD. Although chrome remains the most common faucet finish, true gold tones are gaining in popularity. The unique look connotes luxury and opulence and this faucet finish goes incredibly well with darker—and especially black—kitchen elements, such as the countertop and backsplash tile here. However, you need to consider any gold faucet carefully; they don't work quite as well visually when incorporated into a pure white kitchen.

▶ **APPLY ANTIQUED FINISH FOR A WHOLLY DIFFERENT LOOK.** Antique finishes on faucets are more appropriate for farmhouse sinks and country kitchens. But that's not a rule. You can have an unusual and unique look in your kitchen by adding a modern faucet, such as the gooseneck pictured here, in an antique finish. Surprisingly, the finish fits well with any neutral or white-dominated color scheme.

◀ **UPDATE TRADITIONAL.** The traditional, single-handle, straight spout faucet has served kitchens well for decades. The shape is efficient, and the construction is reliable and durable. It's also subtle but pretty. This updated version in gleaming chrome is as simply handsome as its predecessors, and allows other features—such as solid surface countertops—to take center stage in the kitchen's design.

◀ **INJECT CLASSIC STYLE WITH A GOOSENECK.**
The shape shown here is the time-honored gooseneck faucet that allows for easy cleaning for deeper pots, because the neck arches over the edge of the pot to spray hot water down inside. But the shape is also an elegant form well-suited to accent traditional, country, and period-style kitchen designs. A shiny chrome finish is the classic finish for a gooseneck and the finish of choice if you're adding the faucet to a highly recognizable kitchen theme, such as a cottage kitchen. White enameled handles are a wonderful touch on any chrome faucet, one that also has historical roots.

▼ **DRESS UP CONTEMPORARY WITH A GOOSENECK VARIATION.** This sharp, modern take on the classic gooseneck is minimal, sleek, and a treat for the eye. The smartly curving neck terminates in a pull-down head for ease of cleaning, and the single-lever stylized handle provides ease of use. The best faucets always combine function and style in a package that is undeniably eye-catching and a pleasure to use when it comes time for clean up.

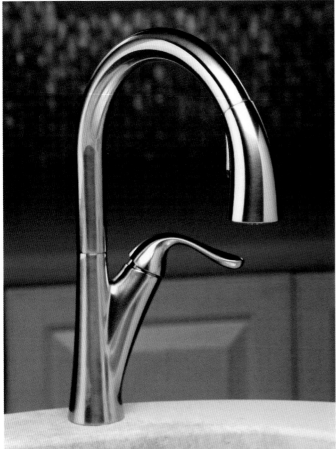

◄ **STICK WITH SIMPLE.** If your kitchen design focuses on uncomplicated lines, plain solid finishes, and lack of patterns, accent it with a basic and beautiful faucet like this understated model. Featuring a proprietary "lustrous metal" finish, this unit has a swooping handle that's easy to grab and a pull-down sprayer head that looks almost seamless with the rest of the neck when not in use. Keep in mind when buying single-hole mount faucets like this that many are offered with optional deck plates, in case you want to install the faucet in a sink or counter with more than one existing hole.

▲ **FIND A FINISH THAT SUITS YOU.** Faucet manufacturers provide more finishes than ever before, and you can choose from conventional chrome to the matte black shown here. This faucet won't show dirt or fingerprints, and it's a standout against the background of a beige quartz countertop and backsplash and brushed metal sink. Picking a faucet finish to contrast other surfaces around it has to be done carefully, but when it works, the look is a surefire hit.

◄ **USE EXISTING CUES TO GUIDE FAUCET CHOICE.** The angular contemporary faucet shown here combines some of the crisp lines and curves of the scintillating backsplash tile, as well as the simple elegance of a solid-colored, solid-surface countertop and plain stainless steel sink. Note how the sink's brushed finish makes the chrome faucet pop just a little bit.

ESTABLISH A PRO LOOK WITH YOUR FAUCET. Do you cook—and consequently clean up—a lot? A professional-quality faucet like this will serve heavy-duty cleanup needs, and brings a "serious kitchen" aesthetic to the sink area. A stainless steel coil neck allows for a lot of flexibility in moving the head around to clean larger or oddly shaped pots and pans. The spray head is multifunction to produce different sprays depending on what you're trying to clean, and a bridge between the body and head helps keep the head steady for hands-free cleaning. It's a look that's all about function, yet presents an enticing form.

▲ **TOUCH AND GO.** This gleaming faucet is the state of the art for kitchen waterworks. Although it has an operable handle, it can also be activated or deactivated by a touch on the body of the faucet—with finger, back of hand, or even the forearm. The automatic water feature can be set to cold water or warm, based on your preference and that glistening chrome finish is protected by a proprietary coating that is both antitarnish and antilime coating. These types of features are common at the current high-end of kitchen faucets.

◄ **FIND A HANDLE WITH FLAIR.** One of the big advances among modern kitchen faucets has been in handle technology. Not only are there a multitude of handle options from which you can choose, they accommodate a wider range of users than ever before and are thoughtful designs that eliminate frustration. For instance, this handle is operated only by turning forward, so that the user never bumps into the backsplash. A simple, yet essential, design feature. The icing on the cake is that the handle has been artfully designed to bring a splash of eye candy to the faucet and sink.

▶ **CHOOSE A FORM THAT SUPPLIES FUNCTION.**
This low-profile, single-handle faucet sports an
aerodynamic shape that is perfectly in keeping
with the ridged-deck enameled sink and green
glass backsplash. But more importantly, the
pull-out head reaches somewhat farther than a
pull-down head on a gooseneck faucet, giving
the homeowner more flexibility in spraying
down dirty counters alongside the sink. There's
always a balance to be struck in choosing a
faucet, between the perfect look and a unit that
serves exactly the way you want it to.

▲ **PICK POT FILLERS FOR FLAIR.** A pot-filler faucet provides an extendable arm to bring water to the stovetop and fill deep pots
for pasta or other dishes. These can be handy in busy or big family kitchens, but they should never be dull. The easiest way to
add a pot filler into the kitchen design is to match the finish to surrounding design elements. The wall-mounted faucet here
was intentionally chosen with a stainless steel finish that works with the backsplash, hood, shelves, and even the stunning
glass tile on the wall. It's an amazingly coordinated look and the pot filler faucet fits right in.

▲ **CONSIDER PROFILE.** Shopping for faucets usually means looking at them from the front. But if you're going to be equipping a sink in an island, it's wise to consider how the faucet looks from the side. This particular design presents a nearly seamless appearance in profile. The pull-down head is perfectly in line with the curving neck and the handle seems to almost disappear into the lines of the body when viewed from the side. It's a small thing, but the small details of a kitchen design can make or break the look.

◀ **CHOOSE LOW-PROFILE FOR CONTEMPORARY.** The more contemporary swan's curve of this faucet is a bit of an edgier look that is right at home with a sliding-glass sink cover featuring an etched design and the high-tech brushed steel sink. This particular faucet is a center post mount, but includes a decorative deck plate that balances out the sweeping look of the neck and head. That feature would also make this a great choice for a preexisting three-hole deck or sink, and the faucet is ideal for any modern or streamlined kitchen.

Swanky Sinks

○●○○○

▶ **EQUIP YOUR SINK FOR SUPER DUTY.** This double-bowl stainless-steel unit has a sturdy top ledge that will stand up to some rough treatment, but the real sell of the sink is the removable drain grates. This means you can pile in dishes, pans, and pots without ever worrying about whether the sink will continue to drain.

▼ **MAXIMIZE ANY SINK'S USEFULNESS WITH OPTIONAL ACCENTS.** The cutting board and dish-draining rack in this sink are custom-made to sit on an inner lip of the sink. This means food prep can be done right over the garbage disposal and dishes can be left to dry over the sink, rather than on a rack over the wood counter. The features can be positioned to wherever is handiest for the user, and they are simply removed and stored when not needed.

◀ **MATCH FAUCET COLOR TO A SOLID SURFACE SINK.** This sink is fabricated right into the structure of the countertop, and the entire surface is a timeless soft white. Solid surface sinks are colored all the way through, so scratches or other marks can be buffed out, and the sink is extremely durable in any case. But this look is especially effective based on the matching faucet. This sleek, single-handle unit has a white body that matches the sink and makes the whole look seamless, minimal, and modern.

▼ **OUTFIT YOUR SINK FOR SPECIAL STORAGE.** You wouldn't think the bowl of a sink could provide storage, but you'd be wrong. With larger stainless steel sinks—especially those in an island or serving as a second sink—the sink may never be used to capacity for cleaning large cookware. Take the opportunity of the extra room to keep sponges, soaps, and other essentials like pot brushes off the countertop. Specialized in-sink containers are offered by several manufacturers to help you work efficiently and keep the sink area tidy.

SINK SHOPPING TIPS

Any time you're looking at new countertops—or a complete kitchen remodel—a new sink should be part of the picture. Of course, you might just be replacing a worn-out sink that's chipped and an eyesore. In any case, follow these tips for sink-shopping success.

- Plan on buying a new strainer body or disposal sleeve, sink clips, and a fresh drain trap kit at the same time as you purchase the new sink.

- Shop for a sink with a basin divider that is lower than the sink rim, to reduce splashing.

- Pick a sink with the drains located near the back wall, to ensure more usable space in the cabinet underneath the sink.

- If you're reusing an existing faucet, measure and check that the holes in the new sink deck match your existing fixture. Or buy the sink first and then purchase a faucet to match the holes.

▲ **MAKE IT MATTE TO DRAW ATTENTION TO YOUR SINK.** A matte sink surface is an eye-catching look in a room where glossy surfaces tend to dominate. Although this sink's finish is matte, it is just as easy to keep clean as its glossier cousins. Keep in mind that the look is a sophisticated contemporary style that most likely won't fit into a period kitchen designs. The sink finish does, however, work quite nicely with a pro-quality faucet like the one shown here.

BUILD A DYNAMIC DUO. This stunning faucet features a coiled steel neck that allows the spray head to be directed where needed, with a lock bar that keeps it in place over the sink when flexibility is not needed. The solid-surface sink includes two bowls and a work surface, all in the same durable material that will stand up to a lot of abuse. The form of the sink accommodates a colander insert and a drain grid, both of which make food prep and cleanup easier. The combination of faucet and sink make preparing gourmet meals a cinch and create a stunning visual for the kitchen.

INCREDIBLE ISLANDS

Island Magic

The kitchen island has become an essential for any kitchen with enough floor space to support one. No wonder, given how useful this piece of furniture can be. Not only does an island offer extra kitchen storage, but it also provides a top surface that can be used for prep or as an additional eating surface.

Dimensions are, of course, the critical factor in considering an island. The most common mistake made with islands is not leaving enough room around the unit for free movement throughout the kitchen. In a big kitchen, that usually means allowing for two people to pass each other on any side of the island. That's why it's always best to create a size-and-shape template from cardboard, and set it on the kitchen floor. It will quickly become apparent if the island overly encroaches into other areas.

Beyond the size, islands allow for a lot of options. Create a breakfast bar ledge with room for stools underneath. And if you're willing to go to the expense and effort, you can take advantage of the most popular trend for islands—plumbing them.

A second sink is incredibly useful for prepping food on the island, or cleaning up when someone else is using the other sink. You can even make the island's sink your primary, and free up counter space in place of a sink along the perimeter of the room. You can also add a cooktop to the island, but that's a major commitment that requires running either a gas line or a high-voltage electrical connection.

If you don't feel inclined to commit to an installed island, you can always add an aftermarket version with legs, or go a step farther and add one with wheels. In either case, make sure the look blends with the rest of the kitchen (or intentionally contrasts it) and you'll still enjoy added space, storage, and utility all in centerpiece for the room.

▼ **MAINTAIN PROPORTION.** Here, a big, bright, white kitchen is well served with a stunning centerpiece island. The island is visually tied to the rest of the room through the use of matching granite countertops. The styling of the base perfectly matches the footed style of the cabinets throughout the kitchen. The size is right, too: the island leaves enough space for navigation but doesn't appear lost in the huge floor space of this kitchen.

MAKE THE ISLAND YOUR NERVE CENTER. Where the layout of the kitchen allows for it, a large island can be ground zero for prep and cleanup. This large island includes a full-size sink and high-end faucet, with a wine cooler built into the base. There is more than enough room to prep any size meal, and the opposite side of the island doubles as a breakfast bar. The positioning leaves plenty of room for people to navigate around the centerpiece.

DON'T FEAR FUNCTION-FREE ISLANDS. Sometimes all you need is a bit more prep surface and a smidge more storage. When that's the case, there's no need to overthink your island. Adding sinks or cooktops usually means new plumbing or electrical work, so an island like this one—with its modest size, simple countertop, and basic combination of one cabinet and open space—can serve perfectly in the kitchen. Styled like the other storage and surfaces in the room, an island like this can blend right into the design while still adding attractive form and furnishing to the kitchen.

CLEAN UP ON AN ISLAND. Because they are usually centrally located, islands are just about the perfect place for a sink— either the primary sink in the kitchen or a smaller ancillary sink for food prep and smaller messes. You do have to run plumbing for the sink, but once the water supply and drain are in place, you have the option of adding in a dishwasher like the one in this island. Take care in choosing a sink and faucet because they'll be on permanent display in the center of the kitchen. A stunning duo like those shown here are well worth the investment.

▲ **MAKE YOUR ISLAND DISTINCTIVE.** You can choose to create a distinctive look with the island in your kitchen, as long as it meshes with the look of the other decorative elements. The impressive island in this kitchen features fine woodworking details and a signature pine grain, but the exceptional wood base marries well with the country-style high-end cabinetry and muted colors in the room. The countertop matches the other countertops in the room, as well as the seats on the stools, and helps tie the look together.

▶ **COMBINE WORK SURFACE AND SINK.** This stunning modern faucet sets off an innovative stainless steel sink design. A durable safety glass panel slides along the top edge of the sink to open and close as needed. When closed, it can be used as a cutting board and neatly conceals the sink. Open, it allows for easy cleanup of food prep by wiping it right into the bowl of the sink. Simple dual-use solutions like this are great in smaller kitchens, where prep space will be at a premium.

ADD PORTABILITY TO INCREASE USEFULNESS. Although most islands are secured to the floor in one way or another, a sturdy wheeled island like this marble-topped wood unit can offer a lot of advantages in the right kitchen. The mobility allows you to put the work surface exactly where you want it at any given time. This can make food prep and cooking much easier. You can also move the island entirely out of the way when you want more room to move around. This style of island is usually less expensive than a built-in unit and, as this example shows, it can still supply plenty of usable storage.

LIGHTING THE KITCHEN DESIGN

Alluring Windows & Skylights

Smart Lighting Fixtures

▼ **BLEND LIGHTING FOR MAXIMUM IMPACT AND TO SET MOOD.** The globe pendants over the island are design stunners and great sources of illumination in this kitchen, but they are far from alone. Undercabinet and undercounter lighting creates subtle illumination, as does cabinet interior lighting. The soft glow creates a lovely mood in the room, and the main lighting fixtures are controlled by a dimmer, allowing the light level to be pumped up when needed.

Light is the most important design element in a kitchen. If you doubt it, just try turning all the lights off some night and see how well the kitchen's design holds up in the dark! But lighting is much more than a simple design element in the kitchen; the proper lighting is crucial in making working, eating, and navigating in the kitchen easier and safer. You can even use lighting to create different moods at different times. Of course, that all depends on what type of light you're working with.

There are two basic types of light in any kitchen: the natural illumination from windows, skylights, and adjacent rooms, and the artificial light from the lighting fixtures. Artificial light can be further broken down into general, or "ambient," light sources, work or task lighting, and accent lighting that highlights specific design features. The best kitchen designs include a balance of all three of these in a design technique called "layering."

Getting that mix right can be made complex by the fact that different light bulbs provide distinctively different types of light. Light fixtures themselves can be largely hidden or become part of the design—sometimes, a big part.

Chances are, your natural light is pretty much determined by the windows you have. You may be able to install a skylight or solar tube, but for the most part, taking advantage of natural light means designing around the sunlight that comes in during the day.

Artificial light, on the other hand, is a design feature that requires just as much thought, consideration, and shopping as any other feature or fixture. In fact, because it's usually fairly easy to swap out light fixtures or locate new artificial lighting, you may find yourself regularly changing your fixtures as a way of updating the look of the kitchen. However, you always want to maintain proper layering of light in the space to maintain safety and comfort. Get your kitchen lighting right, and you'll not only be illuminating the room, you'll be making the design even more beautiful.

SLICE THE SKY. A series of small skylights (these are nonoperable) can pack as much punch as a much larger single unit. These three skylights scatter sunlight across the space during the course of the day and bring as much visual fireworks as a larger single unit would, quite possibly at a lower cost.

▲ **ADD LEADED GLASS FOR A DISTINCTIVE LIGHT-TRANSMITTING DECORATION.** Stained glass is a wonderful accent in the right kitchen, especially one that mixes design influences like the room pictured here. The color in stained glass won't fade or erode, and when used in a detailed window design, the stained glass comes to life when lit (and has an entirely different personality when not illuminated). Because the glass can mute light, it's wise to use a decorative stained-glass window among other windows to maintain adequate levels of sunlight during the day.

▲▶ **LIMIT LIGHT BLOCKING WHEN WINDOWS ARE FEW.** This Euro-style galley kitchen receives moderate direct daylight courtesy of a double-hung window. The homeowner uses a sheer window covering that will ensure privacy when necessary, but won't prevent light transmission even when the shade is down. Keep illumination in mind whenever you are choosing kitchen window treatments.

▶ **FRAME A FAUCET WITH STUNNING WINDOW PAIRS.** The modern faucet in this gorgeous space features a pull-down spray head and universal design lever handle, and it's showcased between two sets of divided-lite casement windows. The window frames have been painted an attractive dark gray, which bridges the ebony floor and lower cabinets and the bright white tile and paint of the walls. Although the windows bring in plenty of light, positioning the faucet right between them creates a central focal point for the room's design.

◀ **BRING THE SUNLIGHT TO THE KITCHEN.** Even if your kitchen isn't directly below the roof, you can route the sunshine to the room with the help of a tubular skylight like the one shown here. These special fixtures use a reflective flexible tube that runs from the roof down as far as necessary to the ceiling of the kitchen. The result is a warm splash of light throughout the day—and you can even add a decorative effect by using one of the special lenses manufacturers offer, such as a prismatic lens.

▼ **CONTROL NATURAL LIGHT.** As lovely as natural light is, sometimes there can be too much of a good thing. A glass door and bank of counter-to-ceiling windows supplies plenty of sunlight during the course of the day, but can also heat up this south-facing kitchen. The answer is simple: Black-out cellular shades that can be raised and lowered with the pull of a cord. Always try to maintain as much control over the natural light in your kitchen as you have over the artificial light.

LIGHT THE SPINE. If you have cathedral ceilings or vaulted construction like this A-frame, a ridge skylight can be an unparalleled lighting and design feature. Although it doesn't appear to take up a lot of the ceiling area, because of the angles, it gathers an abundance of sunlight. And the look is simply incredible; it visually opens up the kitchen during the day and provides a starlit vista at night.

▶ **TILE BACKSPLASHES FOR A BRIGHT WASH OF LIGHT.** Glass tiles can be the perfect choice for backsplashes meant to reflect modest undercabinet lighting fixtures. The simple glass tiles on this backsplash really pop when the undercabinet lights come on, creating a spotlight feature that provides work surface illumination and a pretty visual to boot.

▽ **SELECT CENTERPIECE FIXTURES THAT DOUBLE AS ARTWORK.** Today's lighting manufacturers create stunning light fixtures, many of which would be just as at home in a gallery or museum as they would in a kitchen. These fan-shaped LED fixtures are one of example of lighting as art, and they provide a captivating visual over the island in this kitchen. Of course, their primary function isn't forgotten, and the light they provide is clean, crisp, and well suited to the prep area.

▲ **SPLURGE ON LESS PRACTICAL ISLAND FIXTURES WHERE OTHER FIXTURES AND SOURCES WILL FILL IN ILLUMINATION.** These hexagon wood tubes might not provide blinding light, but they do captivate the kitchen with a unique and charming appeal. They are a great counterpoint to the stunning contemporary faucet with their brushed nickel finishes, and the fixtures complement the wood floor. Reflective surfaces throughout the kitchen work with recessed ceiling lights and other lighting sources to fill in the light in the kitchen.

▲▶ **MAKE USE OF UNDERCABINET SPACE.** Most framed cabinets are constructed with a bottom cavity that is ideal for undercabinet lighting fixtures like these. These simple LED fixtures are the latest technology, offering the option of warmer traditional yellow light, or crisper, task-oriented bright white light at the flip of a switch. They are simple to install, incredibly useful, and a great way to round out your kitchen's illumination plan.

▶ **COMBINE PENDANTS AND TRACK LIGHTS FOR AN ALL-IN-ONE SOLUTION.** These stylish pendants are suspended over an island, but powered by an overhead track that also holds two adjustable track heads. The pendants can be positioned anywhere along the track, as can the two additional heads, providing a great deal of design flexibility. The track also creates a nice curvy graphic overhead, which adds to the impression the bell-shaped pendants make. And, in the end, it's much easier to wire in a single track than three pendants and a track.

▲ **LAYER KITCHEN LIGHTING.** Design experts use the term "layering" to describe the ideal lighting scheme for this busiest of rooms. This means you need to first establish well-dispersed general (or "ambient") lighting, achieved with the ceiling fixtures in this kitchen. Task lighting comes next, illuminating key work areas around the room, as with the lighting pendants over the island cooktop and the undercabinet lights here. Last is the layer of accent lighting that decorates as well as illuminates. The toe-kick, under-counter LEDs, and cabinet lighting all fall into this last category. Combine all the layers and you get a warm, beautifully lit scene like this ideal kitchen.

ALLOW PUCK LIGHTS TO SHOW FOR A TRENDY FEEL. Puck LED lights are often concealed behind the lower ridge of cabinetry face frames, but that's not a hard and fast rule. In fact, exposed puck lights can look quite cool in the right setting. The white fixtures on the left perfectly complement the upscale glass backsplash tiles and blonde cabinetry. The metal pucks on the right give this modern black-and-white kitchen a little extra flare and really bring the shimmering black backsplash tiles to life.

LIGHT RIGHT

Lighting a kitchen can be a tricky affair. Thankfully, interior designers have long used a number of tried-and-true strategies for effectively lighting a very busy space. There's no need to reinvent the wheel—just borrow ideas from the pros!

- **MIX FOR SUCCESS.** Even small kitchens should include an enlightened mix of general ambient lighting, task lighting, and decorative or mood lighting. Don't depend on a single general overhead fixture; any area where people cluster or specific tasks are done should be lit with its own fixtures. This includes general lighting over kitchen tables, above islands, and for the overall floor plan, and specific task lighting over the stove, sink, and prep areas. Decorative cabinet, valance, or toe kick lighting adds dimension to the room and allows you to highlight specific decorative features.

- **ISLANDS AND BREAKFAST BARS.** Use odd numbers of smaller pendants (usually three) or pairs of large pendants. Hang any island pendant so that the bottom of the fixture is 28 to 34 inches above the countertop surface.

- **DINING OR KITCHEN TABLE.** Here's a nifty math trick kitchen designers use when choosing a chandelier size to go over the table. Add the length and width of the room together, rounding up. Convert the sum to inches, and you'll have the size of chandelier that's right for the table. For example, to calculate the chandelier for a 12×14 dining area: 12 + 14 = 26 inches. The bottom of any chandelier should hang 32 to 34 inches above the top of the table.

- **UNDERCABINET.** Mount undercabinet fixtures closer to the front of the cabinet for the best spread of light on the surface below. It's also a great idea to put undercabinet lighting on a dimmer whenever possible; this gives you total control over the kitchen's mood.

▲ **REINTERPRET THE CHANDELIER.** Although the most common lighting for kitchen islands is a series of pendants, the right version of a chandelier can serve the structure well. This rectangular illuminated modern art provides a good amount of light for the surface of the island (augmented by the recessed ceiling fixtures), but it provides a focal point for what was already a stunning kitchen with wood ceiling and patterned tiles.

PICK PENDANTS FOR FORM AS WELL AS LIGHT. The selection of pendant lamps on the market seems almost limitless, and you'll find them in every design style imaginable, and in different materials, from glass to paper to metal and beyond. Although they must first and foremost provide the amount and type of illumination you need wherever you intend to hang them, you can select a style that not only complements the rest of your kitchen design but—as with these three pendants—provides stunning focal points all on their own.

AWESOME EXTRAS

Delightful Accents

Small accents are a way for you to make your kitchen design uniquely your own. These elements may be modest in size, but they can make a big impact on the overall design, and can take a design from simple to chic in a heartbeat. The really good news is that because they are usually inexpensive, accents won't break the bank if you opt for high-end materials and finishes.

The most obvious—and essential—accents are the hardware that goes on cabinets and drawers. Handles, pulls, hinges, and knobs are all design flashpoints that can draw attention to themselves or not. There are so many variations for each of these that the hardest part is sifting through all the options. Choose correctly and these tiny accents can bring new life to old cabinetry.

But accents don't stop at the hardware on your cabinets. Wine racks, small appliances, and even clocks up the ante by incremental degrees, each addition putting a little more polish on your style.

If you're still working on the look of your kitchen or thinking about shifting up the style in one direction another, you can accent the look to make it just right. Just use portable features like glass racks, trays, spice racks, or bowls, which can be swapped out if you decide on a different design direction.

MAKE A BIG IMPACT WITH COLORED KNOBS. You can customize cabinet hardware to suit your needs as the homeowner here has done. This kitchen borders a children's play area in a large kitchen, and the wooden cabinet door knobs, painted in matte primary colors, inject a healthy dose of fun and visual interest. The bright white cabinets, warm vinyl floor (in a surprising diagonal wood plank appearance), and simple wood counters all keep the design honest and ensure that the burst of colors doesn't look jarring or clownish. It's an upbeat, sunny, and happy look full of natural charm.

SURPRISE THE EYE. What looks like a stylish secret cubby hole is actually a chic way to gather recipe trimmings for composting. A compost pile is a great way to feed your garden and help the environment, but collecting kitchen waste has usually been something to hide. Not anymore. This sleek unit pops right into a hole in the countertop, and is covered with a stainless steel lid. When the container gets full, just remove it and take it out to the compost pile. This is a great way to make a design plus out of something that would otherwise be a minus.

RESOURCES

American Standard
Faucets, sinks, and accessories.
www.americanstandard-us.com

Anvil Motion
Universal Design automated cabinetry.
www.anvilmotion.com

Big Chill
Colored appliances and fixtures.
www.bigchill.com
(877) 842-3269

Blanco America
Sinks, faucets, and accessories.
www.blancoamerica.com

Bosch
Kitchen appliances and ventilation.
www.bosch-home.com/us

Cambria
Quartz countertops.
www.cambriausa.com

Canyon Creek Cabinetry
Custom cabinetry.
www.canyoncreek.com
(800) 228-1830

Crown Point Cabinetry
Custom cabinetry.
www.crown-point.com
(800) 999-4994

Elkay Manufacturing Company
Sinks, faucets, and accessories.
www.elkayusa.com

Globus Cork Flooring
Cork flooring.
www.corkfloor.com
(718) 742-7264

Forbo
Marmoleum Click flooring.
www.forbo.com

Formica
Laminate countertops.
www.formica.com

KraftMaid
A full range of cabinetry and cabinetry accessories.
www.kraftmaid.com
(888) 562-7744

Merillat
A full range of cabinetry and cabinetry accessories.
www.merillat.com
(866) 850-8557

National Kitchen & Bath Association
Kitchen planning advice and guidance, listings or professionals, design idea guides.
www.nkba.org
(800) 843-6522

PaperStone
Recycled paper countertops.
www.paperstoneproducts.com
(360) 538-1480

RichLite
Recycled paper countertops.
www.richlite.com
(888) 383-5533

Silestone
Quartz countertops.
www.silestoneusa.com
(866) 268-6837

SMEG
Italian-designed appliances.
www.smegusa.com
(866) 736-7634

Sub-Zero
High-end, restaurant-quality appliances.
www.subzero-wolf.com

Vetrazzo
Recycled-glass countertops.
www.vetrazzo.com

Viking
High-end, restaurant-quality appliances.
www.vikingrange.com

WalkerZanger
Ceramic and stone tile.
www.walkerzanger.com

WilsonArt
Laminate and solid-surface countertops and flooring products.
www.wilsonart.com

PHOTO CREDITS

Page 27 top: Photo courtesy of Bertch Cabinet Manufacturing, www.bertch.com

Page 27 bottom: Photo courtesy of Armstrong Flooring, www.armstrongflooring.com

Page 28 top: Photo courtesy of Snaidero USA, www.snaidero-usa.com, (877) 762-4337

Page 28 bottom: Photo courtesy of Frigidaire, www.frigidaire.com, (800) 374-4432

Page 29 top: Photo courtesy of Kichler, www.kichler.com, (866) 558-5706

Page 29 bottom: Photo courtesy of MasterBrand Cabinets, www.masterbrand.com

Page 30: Photo courtesy of Kichler, www.kichler.com, (866) 558-5706

Page 31 top: Photo courtesy of GE appliances, www.geappliances.com

Page 31 bottom: Photo courtesy of BLANCO, www.blancoamerica.com, 888-668-6201

Page 32 left: Photo courtesy of Wilsonart, www.wilsonart.com, (800) 433-3222

Page 32 right: Photo courtesy of Mannington Mills, Inc. www.mannington.com

Page 33 top: Photo courtesy of Jenn-Air, jennair.com

Page 33 bottom: Photo courtesy of Plain & Fancy Custom Cabinetry, plainfancycabinetry.com

Page 34: Photo courtesy of Kraftmaid, www.kraftmaid.com

Page 35 top: Photo courtesy of Interstyle Ceramic + Glass, www.interstyle.ca, 800-944-2904

Page 35 bottom: Photo courtesy of Brizo Kitchen & Bath Company, www.brizo.com, (877) 345-2749

Page 36 top: Photo courtesy of Armstrong Flooring, www.armstrongflooring.com

Page 36 bottom: Photo courtsey of GROHE, www.grohe.us, (800) 444-7643

Page 37 top: Photo courtesy of Kohler, www.us.kohler.com

Page 37 bottom: Photo courtesy of Bertch Cabinet Manufacturing, www.bertch.com

Page 38: Photo courtesy of MasterBrand Cabinets, www.masterbrand.com

Page 39 top: Photo courtesy of Brizo Kitchen & Bath Company, www.brizo.com, (877) 345-2749

Page 39 bottom: Photo courtesy of Artistic Tile, (877) 237-4097, www.artistictile.com

Page 40 top: Photo courtesy of Kichler, www.kichler.com, (866) 558-5706

Page 40 bottom: Photo courtesy of Kraftmaid, www.kraftmaid.com

Page 41 top: Photo courtesy of Viking, www.vikingrange.com

Page 41 bottom: Photo courtesy of Plain & Fancy Custom Cabinetry, plainfancycabinetry.com

Page 42: Photo courtesy of Kraftmaid, www.kraftmaid.com

Page 43 top: Photo courtesy of Wilsonart, www.wilsonart.com, (800) 433-3222

Page 43 bottom: Photo courtesy of the Solid Wood Cabinet Company, www.solidwoodcabinets.com, 855-277-4820

Page 44 top: Photo courtesy of Poggenpohl, www.poggenpohl.com

Page 44 bottom: Photo courtesy of Formica Corporation, www.formica.com

Page 45 top left: Photo courtesy of BLANCO, www.blancoamerica.com, 888-668-6201

Page 45 bottom left: Photo courtesy of Bosch Home Appliances, www.bosch-home.com/us, 800-944-2904

Page 45 right: Photo courtesy of Top Knobs, www.topknobs.com

Page 46 top: Photo courtesy of Vetrazzo, www.vetrazzo.com

Page 46 bottom: photo courtesy of Cosentino USA, www.silestoneusa.com, 866-268-6837

Page 47 top: Photo courtesy of Kichler, www.kichler.com, (866) 558-5706

Page 47 middle: Photo courtesy of GE appliances, www.geappliances.com

Page 47 bottom: Photo courtesy of Pyrolave, www.pyrolave.fr

Page 48 top: Photo courtesy of Cambria, www.cambriausa.com, 866-CAMBRIA

Page 48 bottom: Photo courtesy of Poggenpohl, www.poggenpohl.com

Page 49 top: Photo courtesy of Brizo Kitchen & Bath Company, www.brizo.com, (877) 345-2749

Page 49 bottom: Photo courtesy of Frigidaire, www.frigidaire.com, (800) 374-4432

Page 50 top: Photo courtesy of Forbo Flooring Systems, www.forbo-flooring.com

Page 50 bottom: Photo courtesy of Interstyle Ceramic + Glass, www.interstyle.ca, 800-944-2904

Page 51: Photo courtesy of Forbo Flooring Systems, www.forbo-flooring.com

Page 52 top: Eric Roth, photographer, www.ericrothphoto.com

Page 52 bottom: Photo courtesy of Kraftmaid, www.kraftmaid.com

Page 53 top: Photo courtesy of Crown Point Cabinetry, www.crown-point.com, 800-999-4994

Page 53 bottom: Photo courtesy of American Standard, www.americanstandard-us.com

Page 54: Photo courtesy of Top Knobs, www.topknobs.com

Page 55: Photo courtesy of Plain & Fancy Custom Cabinetry, plainfancycabinetry.com

Page 56: Photo courtesy of Walker Zanger, Inc., www.walkerzanger.com

page 57 top: Photo courtesy of Crown Point Cabinetry, www.crown-point.com, 800-999-4994

Page 57 bottom left: Photo courtesy of Enclume, www.enclume.com, 877-362-5863

Page 57 bottom right: Photo courtesy of Viking, www.vikingrange.com

Page 58: Photo courtesy of Dewitt Designer Kitchens, www.dewittdesignerkitchens.com, (626) 792-8833

Page 59, all: Photo courtesy of elkay, www.elkay.com

Page 60 top: Photo courtesy of MasterBrand Cabinets, www.masterbrand.com

Page 60 bottom: Photo courtesy of Interstyle Ceramic + Glass, www.interstyle.ca, 800-944-2904

Page 61: Photo courtesy of Vetrazzo, www.vetrazzo.com

Page 62 top: Photo courtesy of Brizo Kitchen & Bath Company, www.brizo.com, (877) 345-2749

Page 62 bottom: Photo courtesy of American Standard, www.americanstandard.com, (800) 442-1902

Page 63 left: Photo courtesy of Bertch Cabinet Manufacturing, www.bertch.com

Page 63 right: Photo courtesy of Top Knobs, www.topknobs.com, (800) 499-9095

Page 64 top left and bottom right: Photo courtesy of Viking, www.vikingrange.com

Page 64 top right and bottom left: photo courtesy of big chill, bigchill.com, 877-842-3269

Page 65, all: Photos courtesy of Smeg, www.smegusa.com

Page 66 top: Photo courtesy of Crown Point Cabinetry, www.crown-point.com, 800-999-4994

Page 66 bottom: Photo courtesy of BLANCO, www.blancoamerica.com, 888-668-6201

Page 67 top: Photo courtesy of Interstyle Ceramic + Glass, www.interstyle.ca, 800-944-2904

Page 67 bottom: Photo courtesy of Pyrolave, www.pyrolave.fr

Page 68 top: Photo courtesy of BLANCO, www.blancoamerica.com, 888-668-6201

Page 68 bottom left: Photo courtesy of Interstyle Ceramic + Glass, www.interstyle.ca, 800-944-2904

Page 69 top: Photo courtesy of Delta Faucet Company, www.deltafaucet.com

Page 69 bottom: Photo courtesy of Richlite, www.richlite.com, 888-383-5533

Page 70: Photo courtesy of Wilsonart, www.wilsonart.com, (800) 433-3222

Page 71, all: Photo courtesy of Cambria USA, www.cambriausa.com

Page 72 top: Photo courtesy of Wilsonart, www.wilsonart.com, (800) 433-3222

Page 72 bottom: Photo courtesy of Cambria USA, www.cambriausa.com

Page 73-74, all: Photo courtesy of Cosentino USA, www.silestoneusa.com, 866-268-6837

Page 75 top: Photo courtesy of American Standard, www.americanstandard-us.com

Page 75 bottom: Photo courtesy of Cambria USA, www.cambriausa.com

Page 76: Photo courtesy of Formica Corporation, www.formica.com

Page 77 top: Photo courtesy of Wilsonart, www.wilsonart.com, (800) 433-3222

Page 77 bottom: Photo courtesy of Formica Corporation, www.formica.com

Page 78, all: Photo courtesy of Formica Corporation, www.formica.com

Page 79 top: Photo courtesy of American Standard, www.americanstandard-us.com

Page 79 bottom: Photo courtesy of Formica Corporation, www.formica.com

Page 80 top: Photo courtesy of Granite Transformations, www.granitetransformations.com

Page 80 bottom left: Photo courtesy of Urban Homes, www.uhny.com

Page 80 bottom right: Photo courtesy of Top Knobs, www.topknobs.com, (800) 499-9095

Page 81: Photo courtesy of iStock

Page 82 top: Photo courtesy of Beth Singer, photographer, www.bethsingerphotographer.com

Page 82 bottom left: Photo courtesy of Dupont Corian, www.dupont.com

Page 82 bottom right: Photo courtesy of Walker Zanger, Inc., www.walkerzanger.com

Page 83 top: Photo courtesy Brooks Custom, www.brookscustom.com, 800-244-5432

Page 83 bottom: Photo courtesy of BLANCO, www.blancoamerica.com, 888-668-6201

Page 84 top: Photo courtesy of Vetrazzo, www.vetrazzo.com

Page 84 bottom: Photo courtesy of J. Gleiberman Design

Page 85: Photo courtesy of Vetrazzo, www.vetrazzo.com

Page 86 left: Photo courtesy of Vetrazzo, www.vetrazzo.com

Page 86 top right: Photo courtesy of Interstyle Ceramic + Glass, www.interstyle.ca, 800-944-2904

Page 86 bottom right: Photo courtesy of Vetrazzo, www.vetrazzo.com

Page 87: Photo courtesy of Cambria USA, www.cambriausa.com

Page 88-89, all: Photo courtesy of Pyrolave, www.pyrolave.fr

Page 90 top: Photo courtesy of Wilsonart, www.wilsonart.com, (800) 433-3222

Page 90 bottom: Photo courtesy of Cambria USA, www.cambriausa.com

Page 91: Photo courtesy Brooks Custom, www.brookscustom.com, 800-244-5432

Page 92 top: Photo courtesy of Richlite, www.richlite.com, 888-383-5533

Page 92 bottom: Photo courtesy of Paneltech/PaperStone®, www.paperstoneproducts.com, 360-538-9815

Page 93 top and bottom left: Photo courtesy of Richlite, www.richlite.com, 888-383-5533

Page 93 bottom right: Photo courtesy of Paneltech/PaperStone®, www.paperstoneproducts.com, 360-538-9815

Page 94 top: Photo courtesy of American Standard, www.americanstandard-us.com

Page 94 bottom: Photo Todd Caverly, architectural photographer, www.toddcaverly.com

Page 95, all: Photo courtesy of Cambria USA, www.cambriausa.com

Page 96: Photo courtesy of GE appliances, www.geappliances.com

Page 97 top: Photo courtesy of Tile of Spain, tileofspainusa.com

Page 97 bottom: Photo courtesy of Snaidero USA, www.snaidero-usa.com, (877) 762-4337

Page 98 top: Photo courtesy of GE appliances, www.geappliances.com

Page 98 bottom: Photo courtesy of Interstyle Ceramic + Glass, www.interstyle.ca, 800-944-2904

Page 99 top: Photo courtesy of Interstyle Ceramic + Glass, www.interstyle.ca, 800-944-2904

Page 99 bottom right: Photo courtesy of Wilsonart International, www.wilsonart.com

Page 99 bottom left: Photo courtesy of Interstyle Ceramic + Glass, www.interstyle.ca, 800-944-2904

Page 100 top: Photo courtesy of GE appliances, www.geappliances.com

Page 100 bottom: Photo courtesy of Livedin Images, www.livedinimages.com

Page 101 top: Photo courtesy of Mannington Mills, Inc. www.mannington.com

Page 101 bottom: Photo courtesy of Armstrong Flooring, www.armstrongflooring.com

Page 102 top: Photo courtesy of Mannington Mills, Inc. www.mannington.com

Page 102 bottom: Photo courtesy of Tile of Spain, tileofspainusa.com

Page 103, all: Photo courtesy of Mannington Mills, Inc. www.mannington.com

Page 104 top: Photo courtesy of GE appliances, www.geappliances.com

Page 104 bottom: Photo courtesy of True Professional Series®, www.true-residential.com

Page 105: Photo courtesy of Forbo Flooring Systems, www.forbo-flooring.com

Page 96 left: Photo courtesy of Armstrong Flooring, www.armstrong.com/flooring

Page 106 top right: Photo courtesy of Karndean Designflooring, www.karndean.com, 886-266-4343

Page 106 bottom: Photo courtesy of Mannington Mills, Inc. www.mannington.com

Page 107 top: Photo courtesy of Mannington Mills, Inc. www.mannington.com

Page 107 bottom: Photo courtesy of Karndean Designflooring, www.karndean.com, 886-266-4343

Page 108, all: Photo courtesy of Armstrong Flooring, www.armstrong.com/flooring

Page 109: Photo courtesy of Globus Cork, www.corkfloor.com, 718-742-7264

Page 110 top: Photo courtesy of Armstrong Flooring, www.armstrong.com/flooring

Page 110 bottom: Photo courtesy of Crown Point Cabinetry, www.crown-point.com, 800-999-4994

Page 111 top: Photo courtesy of Merillat, www.merillat.com

Page 111 bottom: Photo courtesy of Armstrong Flooring, www.armstrong.com/flooring

Page 112 both: Photos courtesy of Mirage Prefinished Hardwood Floors, www.miragefloors.com

Page 113 top: Photo courtesy of Merillat, www.merillat.com

Page 114: Photo courtesy of Bertch Cabinet Manufacturing, www.bertch.com

Page 115 top: Photo courtesy of Photolibrary, www.photolibrary.com

Page 115 bottom: Photo courtesy of the Solid Wood Cabinet Company, www.solidwoodcabinets.com, 855-277-4820

Page 116 top: Photo courtesy of Bertch Cabinet Manufacturing, www.bertch.com

Page 116 bottom: Photo courtesy of the Solid Wood Cabinet Company, www.solidwoodcabinets.com, 855-277-4820

Page 117 top: photo courtesy of Merillat, www.merillat.com

Page 117 bottom left: photo courtesy of Kohler Plumbing, www.kohler.com

Page 117 bottom right: Photo courtesy of Kraftmaid, www.kraftmaid.com

Page 118 both: Photo courtesy of Crown Point Cabinetry, www.crown-point.com, 800-999-4994

Page 119: Photo courtesy of Kraftmaid, www.kraftmaid.com

Page 120 top: Photo courtesy of Formica Corporation, www.formica.com

Page 120 bottom: Photo courtesy of MasterBrand Cabinets, www.masterbrand.com

Page 121 top: Photo courtesy of Plain & Fancy Custom Cabinetry, plainfancycabinetry.com

Page 121 bottom: Photo courtesy of Kraftmaid, www.kraftmaid.com

Page 122 top: Photo courtesy of Kohler, www.us.kohler.com

Page 122 bottom left: Shutterstock

Page 122 bottom right: Photo courtesy of Kohler, www.us.kohler.com

Page 123 top: Photo courtesy of Kraftmaid, www.kraftmaid.com

Page 123 bottom: Photo courtesy of MasterBrand Cabinets, www.masterbrand.com

Page 124-125, all: Photo courtesy of MasterBrand Cabinets, www.masterbrand.com

Page 126: Photo courtesy of Plain & Fancy Custom Cabinetry, plainfancycabinetry.com

Page 127, all: Photo courtesy of Freedom Lift Systems, www.freedomliftsystems.com, 877-947-7769

Page 128 top: Photo courtesy of Merillat, www.merillat.com

Page 128 bottom left: Photo courtesy of Aristokraft Cabinetry Styles, Solutions and more, www.aristokraft.com

Page 128 bottom right: Photo courtesy of Snaidero USA, www.snaidero-usa.com, (877) 762-4337

Page 129 top left: Photo courtesy of Merillat, www.merillat.com

Page 129 top right: Photo courtesy of Snaidero USA, www.snaidero-usa.com, (877) 762-4337

Page 129 bottom: Photo courtesy of Merillat, www.merillat.com

Page 130 top: Photo courtesy of Merillat, www.merillat.com

Page 130 bottom: Photo courtesy of Snaidero USA, www.snaidero-usa.com, (877) 762-4337

Page 131: Photo courtesy of Plain & Fancy Custom Cabinetry, plainfancycabinetry.com

Page 132: Photo courtesy of Merillat, www.merillat.com

Page 133 top: Photo courtesy of Kraftmaid, www.kraftmaid.com

Page 133 bottom: Photo courtesy of Merillat, www.merillat.com

Page 134: Photo courtesy of Armstrong Flooring, www.armstrongflooring.com

Page 135 top: Photo courtesy of Tue Professional Series®, www.true-residential.com

Page 135 bottom: Photo courtesy of Kraftmaid, www.kraftmaid.com

Page 136: Photo courtesy of Siematic, www.siematic.com

Page 137 top and bottom left: Photo courtesy of Enclume, www.enclume.com, 877-362-5863

Page 137 right: iStock

Page 138: Photo courtesy of Armstrong Flooring, www.armstrongflooring.com

Page 139 top: Photo courtesy of IKEA home furnishings, www.ikea.com

Page 139 bottom: Photo courtesy of Richlite, www.richlite.com, 888-383-5533

Page 140: Photo courtesy of Frigidaire, www.frigidaire.com, (800) 374-4432

Page 141: Photo courtesy of Sub-zero, inc., www.subzero-wolf.com

Page 142 top: Photo courtesy of GE appliances, www.geappliances.com

Page 143 top: Photo courtesy of Viking, www.vikingrange.com

Page 143 bottom: Photo courtesy of GE appliances, www.geappliances.com

Page 144 top: Photo courtesy of GE appliances, www.geappliances.com

Page 144 bottom: Shutterstock

Page 145 bottom: Photo courtesy of GE appliances, www.geappliances.com

Page 146 top: Photo courtesy of GE appliances, www.geappliances.com

Page 146 bottom: Photo courtesy of Frigidaire, www.frigidaire.com, (800) 374-4432

Page 147 both: Photo courtesy of GE appliances, www.geappliances.com

Page 148-149, all: Photo courtesy of Viking, www.vikingrange.com

Page 150 top: Photo courtesy of Viking, www.vikingrange.com

Page 150 bottom: Photo courtesy of Wolf Appliance, Inc., www.subzero-wolf.com

Page 151 top: Photo courtesy of Viking, www.vikingrange.com

Page 151 bottom: Photo courtesy of Sub-zero, Inc and Wolf appliance, Inc., www.subzero-wolf.com

Page 152 both: Photo courtesy of True Professional Series®, www.true-residential.com

Page 153: Photo courtesy of Viking, www.vikingrange.com

Page 154 top left: Photo courtesy of Tony Giammarino, photographer, www.tonygiammarino.com

Page 154 top right: Photo courtesy of GE appliances, www.geappliances.com

Page 154 bottom: Photo courtesy of Plain & Fancy Custom Cabinetry, plainfancycabinetry.com

Page 155 left: Photo courtesy of MasterBrand Cabinets, www.masterbrand.com

Page 156 top: Photo courtesy of Walker Zanger, Inc., www.walkerzanger.com

Page 156 bottom: Photo courtesy of Viking, www.vikingrange.com

Page 157 top: Photo courtesy of Artistic Tile, (877) 237-4097, www.artistictile.com

Page 157 bottom: Photo courtesy of Jenn-Air, jennair.com

Page 158: Photo courtesy of Cambria, www.cambriausa.com, 866-CAMBRIA

Page 159 top: Photo courtesy of American Standard, www.americanstandard.com, (800) 442-1902

Page 159 bottom: Photo courtesy of Artistic Tile, (877) 237-4097, www.artistictile.com

Page 160: Photo courtesy of BLANCO, www.blancoamerica.com, 888-668-6201

Page 161: Photo courtesy of Danze, Inc., www.danze.com

Page 162: Photo courtesy of Kallista, www.kallista.com, (888) 452-5547

Page 163-164, all: Photo courtesy of American Standard, www.americanstandard.com, (800) 442-1902

page 165 right: Photo courtesy of American Standard, www.americanstandard.com, (800) 442-1902

page 166: Photo courtesy of Elkay, www.elkay.com

Page 167 top: Photo courtesy of GROHE, www.grohe.us, (800) 444-7643

Page 167 bottom: Photo courtesy of Danze, Inc., www.danze.com

Page 168 top: Photo courtesy of Danze, Inc., www.danze.com

Page 168 bottom: Photo courtesy of Kraftmaid, www.kraftmaid.com

Page 169 top: Photo courtesy of Kohler, www.us.kohler.com

Page 169 bottom: Photo courtesy of American Standard, www.americanstandard.com, (800) 442-1902

Page 170 top: Photo courtesy of American Standard, www.americanstandard.com, (800) 442-1902

Page 170 bottom: Photo courtesy of BLANCO, www.blancoamerica.com, 888-668-6201

page 171 top: Photo courtesy of BLANCO, www.blancoamerica.com, 888-668-6201

Page 171 bottom: Photo courtesy of Elkay, www.elkay.com

Page 172-173, all: Photo courtesy of BLANCO, www.blancoamerica.com, 888-668-6201

Page 174: Photo courtesy of Crown point Cabinetry, www.crown-point.com, 800-999-4994

Page 175 top: Photo courtesy of MasterBrand Cabinets, www.masterbrand.com

Page 175 bottom left: Photo courtesy of Merillat, www.merillat.com

Page 175 bottom right: Photo courtesy of Elkay, www.elkay.com

Page 176 top: Photo courtesy of Crown Point Cabinetry, www.crown-point.com, 800-999-4994

Page 176 bottom: Photo courtesy of Blanco America, www.blancoamerica.com

Page 177: Photo courtesy of Pottery Barn, potterybarn.com, 888-779-5176

Page 178: Photo courtesy of Kichler, www.kichler.com, (866) 558-5706

Page 179: Photo courtesy of Shutterstock

Page 180 top left: Photo courtesy of Viking, www.vikingrange.com

Page 180 top right: Photo courtesy of Kohler Plumbing, www.kohler.com

Page 180 bottom: Photo courtesy of IKEA, www.ikea.com

Page 181 top: Photo courtesy of Solatube, www.solatube.com, 888-Solatube

Page 181 bottom: Photo courtesy of Kichler Lighting, www.kichler.com, 866-558-5706

Page 182: Photo courtesy of Shutterstock

Page 183 top: Photo courtesy of Kichler Lighting, www.kichler.com, 866-558-5706

Page 183 bottom: Photo courtesy of LBL Lighting, www.lbllighting.com

Page 184 top left: Photo courtesy of Delta Faucet Company, www.deltafaucet.com

Page 184 top right: Photo courtesy of Kichler.com, (866) 558-5706

Page 184 bottom right: Photo courtesy of Tiella, www.tiella.com

Page 185: Photo courtesy of Kichler, www.kichler.com, (866) 558-5706

Page 185 bottom left and right: Photo courtesy of Interstyle Ceramic + Glass, www.interstyle.ca, 800-944-2904

Page 186 and 187, all: Photo courtesy of Kichler, www.kichler.com, (866) 558-5706

Page 188: Photo courtesy of Karndean Designflooring, www.karndean.com, 886-266-4343

Page 189 all: Photo courtesy of Blanco America, www.blancoamerica.com